"Love does not consist of gazing at each other, but looking outward together in the same direction."

- Antoine de Saint-Exupéry

Copyright © 2025 by Ethan Starke

All rights reserved. No part of this publication may be reproduced, distributed, or transmitted in any form or by any means, including photocopying, recording, or other electronic or mechanical methods, without the prior written permission of the publisher, except in the case of brief quotations embodied in critical reviews and certain other noncommercial uses permitted by copyright law.

Published by Ethan Starke
5640 Santa Monica Blvd
Los Angeles, California, 90038

ISBN: 979-8-9922475-1-0
First Edition

This book is intended as a practical resource and informational guide. It is not a substitute for professional counseling or therapy. The author and publisher assume no liability for outcomes related to the use of this book.

Curate a Date

Crafting Thoughtful and Creative Experiences for Every Relationship Stage

Preface

Welcome to *Curate a Date*, a book designed to transform how you approach dating. Whether you're navigating the thrill of a first date, keeping the spark alive in a long-term relationship, or simply looking for creative ways to connect, this book offers inspiration and practical guidance.

In today's fast-paced world, creating meaningful experiences can often take a back seat. But the truth is, a thoughtfully planned date can deepen connections, foster understanding, and create lasting memories. This book aims to equip you with the tools, ideas, and confidence to make every date unforgettable.

Curate a Date is more than a list of activities—it's a guide to building intentional, heartfelt moments that reflect who you are and what you value in your relationships. Whether you're adventurers, romantics, food lovers, or artists at heart, you'll find ideas tailored to every mood and stage of connection. Think of this book as your trusted companion, ready to inspire creativity when you need it most.

Dating isn't just about planning something to do; it's about creating opportunities to see and be seen, to listen and share, to laugh and learn together. With the right mindset and a dash of creativity, a simple outing can turn into a memory you both cherish for years to come.

So, let's reimagine what dating can be. From quiet, intimate moments to bold, adventurous experiences, this book invites you to craft dates that matter—to both you and the people you care about. Let's get started!

- Ethan Starke

Introduction

Picture this: You're sitting across from someone you really like, and the conversation is as flat as the room-temperature soda between you. Or maybe, you've planned the perfect date—or so you thought—only to realize you're both allergic to the 'romantic' bouquet-making workshop you booked. If you've ever felt the pressure to create a date that's meaningful, memorable, and maybe even Instagram-worthy, you're not alone.

In a world where swiping right has become the norm, the art of a thoughtful date is often overlooked. But a great date isn't just about avoiding awkward silences or finding the trendiest activity in town. It's about creating a shared experience that brings you closer, fosters understanding, and—let's be honest—makes for a great story to tell later. Whether you're on your first date or your fiftieth, the effort you put into planning can speak volumes about your intentions and your creativity.

This book is your roadmap to becoming a date maestro. It's packed with practical ideas, step-by-step guides, and even fail-safe backup plans for when life—or the weather—throws a curveball. You'll find date concepts tailored for every stage of a relationship, every budget, and every personality. From the romantic to the adventurous, the low-key to the extravagant, *Curate a Date* will help you create moments that matter.

So, are you ready to transform your approach to dating? Let's ditch the generic dinner-and-a-movie routine and start curating dates that truly reflect your unique connection. Because at the end of the day, it's not just about what you do—it's about how you make each other feel.

Imagine this: You've planned what you thought was a perfect hiking date, only to find out your date is terrified of heights. Or perhaps you're at a trendy café, sipping overpriced lattes, and realize you know more about the menu than each other. Sound familiar? The truth is, a date can be much more than an activity—it's an opportunity to build a connection, uncover common ground, and create memories.

Culturally, dating has shifted dramatically over the past decade. Swiping, ghosting, and texting have replaced traditional courtship rituals, often leaving meaningful connection as an afterthought. But here's the thing: humans are wired for connection. Research shows that shared experiences, especially novel ones, release oxytocin—the 'bonding hormone.' In other words, a great date isn't just fun—it's science! Thoughtful planning can foster intimacy, trust, and even adventure.

What Makes a Date Unforgettable?

Think back to the best date you've ever been on. What made it stand out? Was it the place, the activity, or how you felt in the moment? Chances are, it was a combination of these factors. Memorable dates don't happen by accident—they're curated with care. An unforgettable date balances effort, surprise, and personal touch. This book will teach you how to create that perfect balance.

Throughout this book, you'll find date ideas that cater to every type of relationship and personality. Are you a thrill-seeker? There's a chapter for adventurous dates. Looking for something low-budget yet meaningful? We've got you covered. You'll also discover tips on handling date anxiety, rescuing a date that's going off the rails, and even planning virtual dates for long-distance connections. Whether you're new to dating or a seasoned partner, there's something here for you.

What This Book is Not

This isn't a book of generic advice or cookie-cutter solutions. It's not about impressing someone with extravagance or pretending to be someone you're not. Instead, it's about authenticity, creativity, and understanding what makes your connection unique. No two people are the same, and no two dates should be either.

By the time you finish this book, you'll have all the tools you need to create dates that leave a lasting impression. The only question left is: Are you ready to take your dating game to the next level? Let's get started on this journey together.

The Date That Changes Everything

Every great relationship has that one defining moment—the date where everything just clicks. Maybe it was a spontaneous road trip, a cozy night in, or a surprise activity that revealed something unexpected about each other. These moments don't just happen—they're crafted. And the magic lies in the details: the thoughtfulness of the plan, the shared laughter, and the connection that deepens with every passing hour.

Breaking the Mold

Why settle for the ordinary when extraordinary is just a little creativity away? Too often, we fall into dating ruts, repeating the same dinner-and-a-movie routine because it feels safe. But stepping outside your comfort zone can lead to incredible surprises. Imagine swapping out that predictable dinner reservation for a cooking class where you make each other's favorite dish. Or replacing a walk in the park with a treasure hunt in your city. This book will show you how to infuse every date with that extra bit of wonder.

Small Efforts, Big Impact

The beauty of a curated date is that it doesn't have to be grand to be meaningful. A handwritten note hidden in plain sight, a playlist of songs that remind you of each other, or even a last-minute coffee date with an unexpected twist—these small gestures speak volumes. Through this book, you'll learn that it's the thought behind the gesture, not its scale, that leaves a lasting impression.

A Note on Authenticity

At its core, dating is about connection. But connection can only flourish where authenticity exists. This book is a guide, not a rulebook. The ideas here are meant to inspire, not prescribe. The best dates are the ones that feel genuine to you and your partner. So, as you dive into these pages, remember: the goal isn't perfection—it's presence, thoughtfulness, and joy.

As you turn the page, you're not just reading a book—you're embarking on an adventure. Every chapter is a step closer to creating the kinds of dates that aren't just memorable but transformative. Let's leave the ordinary behind and start building the extraordinary together.

Why We Date

Dating isn't just a modern phenomenon—it's a timeless ritual of connection. Throughout history, from ballroom dances to handwritten love letters, people have sought meaningful ways to connect. In today's world, the pace of life has accelerated, and with it, our methods of meeting and bonding have transformed. Yet, the core reason remains unchanged: to find, nurture, and celebrate relationships that bring us joy and fulfillment.

The Power of Shared Experiences

Science tells us that shared experiences can create bonds that go beyond the surface. It's not just about what you do—it's about doing it together. Whether it's the thrill of solving a puzzle in an escape room or the quiet intimacy of watching the sunset, these moments build a foundation of trust, understanding, and affection. Through this book, you'll discover how to turn ordinary activities into extraordinary memories.

Overcoming the Fear of Planning

Planning a date can sometimes feel daunting. What if they don't like it? What if something goes wrong? Here's a secret: perfection isn't the goal. Dates are about connection, not flawless execution. A rainy picnic can turn into an impromptu indoor feast. A missed reservation can lead to a spontaneous adventure. The key is to embrace the unexpected and focus on the joy of being together.

The Ingredients of a Great Date

Every great date has a recipe: a dash of creativity, a pinch of effort, and a generous helping of thoughtfulness. Here's what you'll need:

- **Location**: A setting that complements the vibe you want to create.
- **Activity**: Something that resonates with both of your interests.
- **Connection**: Space for conversation and shared moments.

Throughout this book, you'll learn how to mix and match these ingredients to craft dates that feel special and authentic.

Why This Book Matters Now

In a world dominated by screens and schedules, taking time to curate a meaningful date is more important than ever. This book isn't just about romance—it's about reclaiming the art of human connection. Whether you're looking to reignite a spark, impress a crush, or simply explore new ways to bond, the tools and ideas here are your guide to building relationships that last.

Now that you're equipped with the 'why,' it's time to dive into the 'how.' Let's explore the endless possibilities for creating dates that don't just fill your calendar but enrich your life. Together, we'll turn every outing into an opportunity to connect, grow, and celebrate love in all its forms.

Dating is as much about discovery as it is about connection. At its core, dating allows us to explore who we are in relation to another person. It's a space to uncover shared values, test compatibility, and even challenge our own boundaries. Whether you're embarking on a first date or celebrating decades of togetherness, the act of dating keeps relationships vibrant and alive. It's a dance of curiosity, vulnerability, and shared joy—a ritual that transcends time.

What makes shared experiences so impactful? It's the emotions they evoke—excitement, laughter, surprise, or even the thrill of overcoming a challenge together. Psychologists suggest that when we experience heightened emotions with someone, our brains form stronger connections to them. Think about it: you're more likely to remember the adrenaline rush of a zip-lining date than a standard coffee outing. This book is designed to help you harness the power of shared experiences, creating dates that leave both your hearts racing and your minds connecting.

Let's address the elephant in the room: planning a date can be intimidating. But here's the good news—it doesn't have to be perfect to be meaningful. Start with the basics: choose a location that feels right, plan an activity that sparks interest, and focus on creating a moment of connection. Remember, it's the effort that counts, not the extravagance. A great date isn't about impressing someone; it's about making them feel seen and valued. In the chapters ahead, you'll find plenty of ideas to help you overcome any hesitation and plan with confidence.

In an era of endless notifications and jam-packed schedules, finding time for connection can feel like an uphill battle. Yet, it's precisely in these moments of busyness that intentional dating becomes a lifeline. Whether it's carving out time for your partner, exploring a new connection, or even rediscovering yourself through the lens of a relationship, this book is your compass. Each chapter is a call to slow down, engage, and celebrate the beautiful complexity of human relationships.

As we embark on this journey together, remember: dating is not a task to check off but an opportunity to create magic. Every date has the potential to be a chapter in your story, a moment that shapes your connection. So, grab a pen, take notes, and let's curate some unforgettable dates.

The Fundamentals of a Great Date

What makes a date truly unforgettable? Is it the setting, the activity, or the chemistry between two people? The truth is, it's a mix of all these elements working together seamlessly. Great dates aren't about perfection—they're about crafting moments that feel genuine, engaging, and memorable. In this chapter, we'll uncover the essential building blocks of a successful date, giving you the tools to create experiences that resonate deeply with your partner.

At the heart of any exceptional date lies a balance between intention and spontaneity. It's not just about the plan you make but the effort, creativity, and care you put into it. From understanding the nuances of your partner's preferences to creating an atmosphere that feels just right, this chapter explores how small, thoughtful details can transform an ordinary outing into something extraordinary. You'll learn how to avoid common pitfalls, embrace spontaneity, and set the stage for meaningful connections.

By the end of this chapter, you'll have a clear framework for planning dates that go beyond the ordinary. Whether it's a first date, a long-awaited night out, or a simple evening spent together, these principles will ensure your efforts shine, leaving both of you with memories to cherish. Let's dive into the fundamentals and start crafting the kinds of dates that truly stand out.

The Golden Triangle of a Date

When planning a great date, it all comes down to three core elements: fun, connection, and comfort. These pillars form what we call 'The Golden Triangle of a Date.' Strike the right balance between them, and you've got a recipe for a memorable experience.

Fun

Fun is the spark that makes a date feel effortless and exciting. It's the laughter shared over a quirky board game, the thrill of trying something new together, or the simple joy of being in each other's company. Fun doesn't have to be extravagant—it can be as small as sharing a favorite joke or finding joy in the little moments.

Connection

Connection is the glue that turns a good date into a great one. It's about fostering moments where you truly see and hear each other. This could mean engaging in meaningful conversation, sharing personal stories, or even enjoying a comfortable silence. Connection grows when both people feel valued and understood.

Comfort

Comfort sets the foundation for everything else. If one or both of you feels uneasy—whether it's because of the location, activity, or atmosphere—it's hard to enjoy the date. Prioritizing comfort doesn't mean avoiding adventure; it means creating a space where both people feel at ease enough to be themselves.

A successful date combines these three elements seamlessly. Imagine this: You plan a sunset picnic at a nearby park. The fun comes from playing a lighthearted trivia game while you eat. The connection builds as you talk about your favorite memories tied to sunsets. And the comfort is in the cozy blankets and pillows you brought, ensuring the setting feels warm and inviting. The Golden Triangle isn't about perfection—it's about finding the right balance for the moment.

Know Your Audience

One of the most critical steps in planning a successful date is understanding the person you're sharing it with. This goes beyond knowing their favorite color or food—it's about grasping what makes them feel excited, valued, and comfortable. In short, it's about tailoring the experience to their personality and preferences.

The Importance of Observation

Pay attention to the little things they say and do. Are they an adventurous spirit who lights up at the idea of skydiving, or do they prefer quieter moments like a serene stroll by the lake? Listening to their stories and noticing their reactions to certain ideas can give you all the clues you need to plan a date they'll love.

Asking the Right Questions

Don't be afraid to ask open-ended questions that give you insight into their preferences. Try something like, 'If you could plan your perfect day, what would it look like?' or 'What's something you've always wanted to try but never have?' These questions not only show your interest but also help you gather ideas without being too direct.

The Love Language Factor

Understanding their love language—whether it's words of affirmation, acts of service, receiving gifts, quality time, or physical touch—can make your date incredibly meaningful. For instance, someone whose love language is quality time might value an uninterrupted evening together, while someone who appreciates acts of service might love a surprise homemade dinner.

Here's how knowing your audience can transform a date: Imagine your partner loves art and has mentioned wanting to learn painting. Instead of a standard dinner date, you sign both of you up for a couples' painting class. Not only does this show that you've listened and paid attention, but it also creates an opportunity for shared fun and connection. When you understand what makes your date tick, every outing feels personal and thoughtful.

The Role of Creativity

In a world filled with predictable dinner dates and generic plans, creativity is your secret weapon for making a date unforgettable. Creativity isn't about being over-the-top; it's about adding a unique twist that turns an ordinary outing into an extraordinary experience.

Think Outside the Box

Creativity starts with reimagining the ordinary. For instance, instead of a simple coffee date, why not try a coffee-tasting tour where you explore local cafés? Or replace a movie night at home with a DIY outdoor cinema experience in your backyard. The key is to add a layer of thoughtfulness and fun that stands out.

Tailoring to Interests

A creative date idea often stems from understanding your partner's interests and using them as inspiration. If they love nature, plan a picnic hike with a scenic view. If they're a foodie, organize a mini food tour where you visit several restaurants for appetizers, mains, and dessert. Tailored creativity makes the date feel personal and special.

Adding a Surprise Element

A sprinkle of surprise can elevate your date from good to unforgettable. This doesn't mean you need a grand gesture—small surprises work just as well. For example, you could create a playlist of songs that remind you of your partner and play it during the drive to your destination, or bring along a small, thoughtful gift tied to the theme of the date.

Imagine this scenario: Your date has mentioned loving stargazing but never having the chance to do it properly. You plan an evening picnic under the stars, complete with a telescope and a stargazing app to identify constellations together. This combination of thoughtfulness and creativity makes the experience one they'll never forget. Creativity doesn't have to be complicated—it's about showing effort and thinking beyond the usual.

The Power of Intentionality

In the world of dating, intentionality is a game-changer. It's about making deliberate choices that show your thoughtfulness and care. An intentional date goes beyond just picking a time and place—it's about considering how every detail contributes to the experience.

Understanding What Matters

An intentional date starts with asking yourself a simple question: What will make this person feel valued? Intentionality is less about grandeur and more about meaning. If they've mentioned being overwhelmed at work, an evening of relaxation—like a spa night at home—might mean more than an elaborate outing. Intentionality is about tuning into their current needs and desires.

Personalizing the Experience

A personalized touch can transform even the simplest activity into something special. For example, if your date loves baking, a surprise baking class can be far more meaningful than a generic dinner. Intentionality is in the details—choosing activities, locations, or themes that resonate with your partner's unique preferences.

Demonstrating Effort

Effort speaks volumes in the language of love. Planning ahead, adding thoughtful touches, and considering logistics all show that you've invested time and energy. It's as simple as bringing their favorite snack for a movie night or researching an activity they've mentioned in passing. The effort doesn't have to be huge; it just has to be sincere.

Here's an example: Your date has been dreaming of visiting Paris someday. While a trip to France might not be feasible, you can bring a piece of Paris to them. Set up a mini Parisian picnic with French pastries, a bottle of wine, and some soft jazz playing in the background. The intentionality behind recreating their dream shows thoughtfulness and care.

Overcoming Common Pitfalls

Even with the best intentions, dates don't always go as planned. From logistical hiccups to mismatched expectations, there are plenty of ways things can go off track. But here's the good news: with a little preparation and flexibility, you can navigate these challenges gracefully and turn potential pitfalls into memorable moments.

Avoiding Overplanning

While it's important to have a plan, overloading the agenda can leave little room for spontaneity. A jam-packed schedule can feel more like a marathon than a date. Instead, aim for a balance—plan one or two main activities and leave space for organic moments to unfold.

Communicating Expectations

Miscommunication is one of the most common pitfalls in dating. Make sure you're on the same page about the date's purpose and tone. Is this a casual outing or something more formal? Clarifying these details in advance can prevent misunderstandings and set the right tone for the evening.

Handling Logistics with Care

Logistical issues—like running late, getting lost, or discovering a venue is closed—can derail even the best-laid plans. Double-check details like opening hours, directions, and reservations beforehand. If something does go wrong, stay calm and embrace the opportunity for spontaneity.

Embracing the Unexpected

Not everything will go according to plan, and that's okay. Sometimes, the most memorable dates are the ones where you adapt to unexpected circumstances. If it rains on your picnic, turn it into an indoor picnic at home. If a restaurant mix-up happens, laugh it off and explore a new spot together. Flexibility can turn mishaps into magic.

Here's an example of turning a pitfall into an opportunity: You've planned an outdoor movie night, but a sudden storm rolls in. Instead of calling it off, you rearrange your living room with cozy blankets and snacks, recreating the experience indoors. The effort to adapt not only salvages the date but also shows your willingness to make the best of any situation.

The Role of Atmosphere

Atmosphere can make or break a date. It's the invisible force that sets the tone, shapes the mood, and creates a sense of place. Crafting the right atmosphere isn't about extravagance—it's about intentionality. From lighting and music to location and timing, every detail plays a part in creating an environment that feels just right.

Choosing the Right Location

The setting of a date has a powerful impact on the overall experience. A cozy café might encourage meaningful conversation, while an outdoor adventure sparks excitement. Consider the vibe you're aiming for—intimate, adventurous, casual—and select a location that aligns with that energy.

Setting the Mood with Lighting and Music

Subtle elements like lighting and music can transform a date's atmosphere. Soft lighting creates intimacy, while natural sunlight adds warmth and positivity. Music can serve as a backdrop that enhances the experience, whether it's a live performance, a curated playlist, or the ambient sounds of nature.

Timing is Everything

Timing can elevate a date from good to unforgettable. A sunrise hike brings a sense of renewal, while a sunset picnic feels magical and serene. Think about how the time of day aligns with your chosen activity and the energy you want to create.

Personalizing the Details

Adding personal touches to the atmosphere can make the experience even more special. For example, if your date loves flowers, bring a bouquet to brighten the setting. If they're a movie buff, create a themed setup for a film night. These small details show thoughtfulness and make the atmosphere feel uniquely theirs.

Imagine this: You've planned a rooftop dinner for your date. The lighting comes from string lights and candles, casting a warm glow. Soft jazz plays in the background, and the city skyline provides a stunning view. The atmosphere you've created turns a simple dinner into an unforgettable experience. By paying attention to these details, you ensure the environment enhances the connection between you.

Balancing Spontaneity and Structure

Great dates strike a delicate balance between planning and leaving room for spontaneity. While a well-structured plan shows thoughtfulness, allowing space for the unexpected keeps the experience dynamic and memorable. Too much structure can feel rigid, while too much spontaneity can lead to chaos. Finding the sweet spot is key to creating an enjoyable and relaxed date.

Plan the Framework, Not Every Detail

Start with a clear framework for the date—know the main activity, location, and timing—but avoid overloading it with minute details. This leaves room for natural moments to emerge, like stumbling upon a street performance or taking an impromptu detour for dessert.

Embrace the Unexpected

Spontaneity doesn't mean abandoning the plan entirely; it means being open to the opportunities that arise in the moment. If your date expresses interest in something unplanned—like stopping to admire a sunset or trying a food truck you pass by—embrace it. These moments often become the most cherished memories.

Read the Room

Spontaneity works best when it aligns with your date's mood and energy. If they seem tired, pivot to something more relaxed. If they're excited and adventurous, lean into unplanned opportunities. Paying attention to their cues ensures your spontaneity feels considerate rather than overwhelming.

Have a Backup Plan

While spontaneity is important, it's always good to have a backup plan. If your original idea falls through—like a canceled event or unexpected weather—having an alternative ready shows your adaptability and thoughtfulness. A backup plan doesn't stifle spontaneity; it supports it by keeping the date on track.

Imagine this scenario: You've planned a day trip to a nearby town, complete with a visit to an art gallery and lunch at a cozy café. But while walking through the town square, you stumble upon a live music performance. Instead of rushing to stick to the schedule, you decide to stay and enjoy the music. This balance of planning and spontaneity creates a date that feels both thoughtful and free-flowing.

Putting It All Together

As we close this chapter, let's revisit the essentials that form the foundation of a great date. The Golden Triangle—fun, connection, and comfort—remains your guiding compass, ensuring your date strikes the perfect balance. Knowing your audience allows you to tailor each experience to their unique preferences, while creativity and intentionality add those special touches that make a date unforgettable.

We've also explored how to navigate common pitfalls with grace, create the right atmosphere, and find harmony between structure and spontaneity. Each of these elements plays a vital role in crafting dates that are meaningful, memorable, and uniquely yours.

The beauty of these principles lies in their flexibility—they're tools you can adapt to any situation or stage of a relationship. Whether you're planning a first date, celebrating a milestone, or simply enjoying quality time together, these fundamentals will ensure your efforts shine.

Now that you've got a strong foundation, it's time to dive deeper into specific types of dates and how to make them truly stand out. In the next chapter, we'll explore the art of romantic and intimate dates, uncovering the secrets to creating moments that resonate with love and connection. Let's keep building on this journey together.

Categories of Dates

Not all dates are created equal. The key to a great date lies in tailoring the experience to the occasion, the relationship stage, and the unique preferences of both people involved. In this chapter, we'll explore a variety of date categories that cater to different needs—from romantic and intimate moments to adventurous outings, budget-friendly ideas, and more. These categories serve as a guide to help you create dates that resonate deeply and leave lasting memories.

Romantic and Intimate Dates

For rekindling romance, celebrating milestones, or enhancing intimacy. Examples: Sunset picnics, candlelit dinners at home, stargazing, love letter writing workshops.

Adventurous Dates

For thrill-seekers and those looking to spice up their routine. Examples: Escape rooms, hot air balloon rides, zip-lining, scavenger hunts.

Low-Budget Dates

For creativity without spending much. Examples: DIY movie nights, free museum days, park workouts, volunteering together.

Family-Inclusive Dates

For blending family time with romance. Examples: Group cooking classes, family game nights, outdoor hikes.

Virtual and Long-Distance Dates

For staying connected despite physical distance. Examples: Online painting sessions, virtual escape rooms, synchronized movie streaming.

Self-Care and Wellness Dates

For couples who prioritize health and mindfulness. Examples: Couples' yoga, spa nights at home, outdoor meditation retreats.

Culturally Immersive Dates

For exploring new traditions and cuisines. Examples: Food festivals, dance classes, cultural cooking nights.

Seasonal and Holiday Dates

For making the most of specific times of the year. Examples: Pumpkin patch visits, holiday light tours, summer beach bonfires.

Romantic and Intimate Dates

Romance isn't a one-size-fits-all concept. What feels romantic to one person might not resonate with another, and that's the beauty of creating intimate moments—they can be as unique as the people involved. Whether it's a grand candlelit dinner or a quiet evening spent stargazing, the essence of romance lies in thoughtfulness and connection. In this chapter, we'll explore how to craft dates that deepen bonds and leave a lasting impression of love and care.

True intimacy is built on more than just grand gestures; it's found in the quiet moments of vulnerability, the shared laughter, and the attention to small details that show you truly see and value your partner. From setting the right atmosphere to embracing shared experiences that heighten connection, this chapter is your guide to creating romantic moments that feel genuine and unforgettable.

As we delve into the art of romantic and intimate dates, you'll discover modern twists on timeless classics, creative ideas for adding personal touches, and ways to create memorable experiences regardless of budget. By the end of this chapter, you'll be equipped to plan dates that aren't just romantic but truly meaningful, setting the stage for deeper emotional and physical connections. Let's start crafting the kind of romance that lingers long after the date is over.

The Meaning of Romance

Romance is more than roses and candlelit dinners—it's an expression of care, creativity, and connection. What feels romantic isn't defined by societal norms but by the unique preferences of the people involved. At its core, romance is about making someone feel cherished and understood, often through thoughtful gestures or shared experiences.

In today's fast-paced world, romance has evolved to reflect more personal and authentic expressions of love. While traditional symbols of romance like flowers and fine dining still hold their charm, modern romance often emphasizes effort and intention. A handwritten note, a playlist curated with their favorite songs, or a day spent exploring a shared passion can feel just as, if not more, meaningful.

Romance doesn't have to follow a script. For some, a quiet night binge-watching their favorite series feels more romantic than a formal date night. For others, an adventurous day spent hiking and stargazing might be the ultimate gesture of love. By stepping away from clichés and embracing what feels genuine to your relationship, you can create moments that truly resonate.

Romance isn't about grand gestures or picture-perfect dates—it's about the feeling you create. Whether it's a quiet moment of connection or a day full of surprises, the most romantic dates are those that reflect your unique bond. In this chapter, we'll explore how to take these principles and turn them into unforgettable experiences.

The Role of Ambiance

Ambiance is the silent partner of romance. It sets the tone, evokes emotions, and creates a canvas for connection. From lighting and music to the choice of location, every detail contributes to an atmosphere that feels magical and memorable. In this section, we'll explore how to master the art of ambiance to elevate your romantic dates.

The right setting can transform even the simplest activity into an unforgettable experience. Think about what makes the environment feel intimate and inviting—it could be a quiet park under a canopy of stars, a cozy living room with soft blankets and candles, or a beachside spot where the sound of waves enhances the mood. Tailor the setting to your partner's preferences and the vibe you want to create.

Lighting and music are subtle but powerful tools for creating ambiance. Dim lighting, candles, or fairy lights can add warmth and intimacy, while natural sunlight can make daytime dates feel cheerful and uplifting. Music acts as an emotional backdrop—curate a playlist that reflects the tone of the date, whether it's soft jazz, acoustic melodies, or a collection of songs with personal significance.

What makes ambiance truly special are the personal touches you add. If your partner loves books, set up a date in a cozy library or create a book-themed picnic. If they're a fan of the outdoors, bring elements of nature into the date—like fresh flowers, a homemade trail mix, or even a blanket spread near a scenic view. These details show thoughtfulness and make the date feel uniquely tailored.

Imagine this: You've planned an evening at home, but instead of defaulting to takeout and a movie, you transform the living room into a romantic haven. Candles flicker on the table, soft instrumental music plays in the background, and a home-cooked meal is ready to be shared. The ambiance you've created turns a simple evening in into a heartfelt and unforgettable experience.

Classic Romance, Reimagined

Some romantic gestures are timeless for a reason—they resonate deeply and create moments of connection. But even the classics can benefit from a fresh twist, tailored to modern tastes and personal preferences. Reimagining these staples of romance allows you to honor tradition while making the experience uniquely yours.

A dinner date doesn't have to mean a fancy restaurant. Instead, consider cooking together at home, creating a meal that reflects both of your tastes. Or, turn the traditional dinner date into a progressive experience by visiting different restaurants for appetizers, mains, and dessert. The key is to infuse creativity and shared effort into the experience.

Flowers are a classic romantic gesture, but why not go beyond the bouquet? Consider gifting a potted plant they can nurture, or even creating a small herb garden together. When it comes to gifts, personalization is key—write a heartfelt note, choose a book you know they'll love, or make something meaningful by hand.

Grand romantic gestures don't have to feel outdated or over-the-top. A private concert could be as simple as playing their favorite song on a guitar or sharing a playlist you made just for them. Thoughtful, personal touches turn traditional grand gestures into intimate moments of connection.

For example, instead of just presenting a bouquet of flowers, imagine surprising your partner with a picnic in a park where you plant wildflower seeds together. Or, take the classic serenade idea and adapt it to your skills—a simple voice memo of you singing a favorite song can be just as touching as a live performance. These reimagined classics prove that romance isn't about how much you spend or how extravagant the gesture, but how heartfelt and personal it feels.

Surprise and Delight

There's a special kind of magic in being surprised, especially when the surprise reflects thoughtfulness and care. Surprises don't have to be grand or elaborate—they just need to show that you've been paying attention and put effort into making your partner feel special. In this section, we'll explore the art of crafting surprises that leave a lasting impression.

Sometimes, it's the smallest gestures that carry the most meaning. A handwritten note slipped into their bag, a surprise coffee delivery at work, or a playlist of songs that remind you of them can make their day feel extraordinary. These little surprises are easy to execute but powerful in showing thoughtfulness.

Surprising your partner with an unplanned activity can add excitement and spontaneity to a date. For example, you might plan a mystery outing where they don't know the destination until you arrive. Or, you could coordinate a scavenger hunt with clues that lead to your planned activity. The anticipation and novelty make the surprise even more memorable.

The best surprises are the ones that feel deeply personal. If your partner has mentioned a dream destination, you could create a themed date around that place—like an Italian dinner and gelato for someone dreaming of Rome. Incorporating details that reflect their personality and interests ensures the surprise resonates on a deeper level.

Imagine this: Your partner has always wanted to try pottery but hasn't had the chance. One day, you surprise them with a private pottery class, complete with a keepsake you create together. The surprise itself is thoughtful, but the shared experience adds another layer of connection. When done right, surprises can be the highlight of any romantic relationship.

Shared Vulnerability

True intimacy is built on trust and vulnerability. Sharing your hopes, fears, dreams, and even your quirks creates a deeper connection between you and your partner.

Romantic dates that encourage openness and understanding can strengthen your bond and lay the foundation for long-lasting intimacy.

Vulnerability flourishes in an environment where both people feel safe and valued. Choose settings that foster comfort and openness—a quiet park, a cozy corner of a café, or even your living room. Let the atmosphere encourage honest conversations without judgment.

Certain activities naturally lend themselves to moments of vulnerability. For example, try a question-based game like 'We're Not Really Strangers,' which is designed to deepen understanding. You could also share a meaningful experience, like volunteering together, which can bring out your values and emotions.

Vulnerability is a two-way street. By sharing your own stories, feelings, or insecurities, you invite your partner to do the same. Start small—talk about a challenge you've overcome, a goal you're working towards, or a memory that shaped you. When you lead with vulnerability, it builds trust and encourages your partner to open up as well.

For instance, imagine sitting by a campfire during a quiet evening. You take the opportunity to share a story about a defining moment in your life, and in turn, your partner opens up about their own experiences. These moments of shared vulnerability foster a connection that goes beyond surface-level conversations, creating a bond rooted in understanding and trust.

Incorporating Sensory Experiences

Romantic dates that engage the senses leave a lasting impression. By thoughtfully including sensory elements, you can create experiences that feel immersive and memorable. Whether it's the scent of fresh flowers, the texture of a picnic blanket, or the taste of a carefully chosen dish, engaging the senses adds depth and richness to your date.

Food and drink are natural ways to engage the senses of taste and smell. Plan a wine or cheese tasting, bake cookies together, or visit a local market to sample fresh produce. For added impact, choose flavors and aromas that evoke nostalgia or hold personal significance for your partner.

The visual and auditory elements of a date can shape the overall experience. Think about the colors, lighting, and décor of your setting, as well as the sounds that accompany it. For instance, you could plan a date at an art gallery or set up an outdoor movie night with a custom playlist to complement the mood.

The sense of touch is often overlooked but plays a key role in creating intimacy. Share a dance, hold hands during a walk, or plan an activity like pottery where physical engagement is central. These moments of tactile connection can enhance the feeling of closeness.

Imagine planning a date that engages all five senses: a cozy picnic in the park with aromatic candles, delicious snacks, a soft blanket, beautiful surroundings, and your favorite music playing in the background. By thoughtfully engaging the senses, you create an experience that is not only enjoyable in the moment but lingers in memory long after the date is over.

Romance on a Budget

Romantic dates don't have to come with a hefty price tag. In fact, some of the most meaningful moments come from creativity and thoughtfulness rather than extravagant spending. This section explores ways to create romantic experiences that are rich in connection but light on the wallet.

Take advantage of activities that cost little to nothing but offer a wealth of enjoyment. A walk through a scenic trail, a visit to a free museum day, or stargazing from your backyard can all be incredibly romantic. The key is to focus on the quality of the experience rather than the cost.

Put your own spin on romance with do-it-yourself date ideas. Cook a special meal together at home, build a blanket fort for a cozy movie night, or create handmade gifts for each other. DIY dates show effort and thoughtfulness, proving that romance isn't about what you buy but what you build together.

Look around your community for budget-friendly options. Many towns offer free concerts, farmers' markets, or outdoor movie nights that can make for unique date experiences. Exploring your local area not only saves money but can also create a deeper connection to the place you share.

For example, imagine planning a day of simple but meaningful activities: start with a morning hike at a nearby trail, pack a picnic lunch with homemade sandwiches, and end the day watching the sunset from a scenic overlook. These moments of connection don't require a large budget, just a little thought and care.

Capturing the Essence of Romance

Romance is not about the size of the gesture or the money spent; it's about the thought, care, and connection that goes into the experience. From reimagining classic date ideas to crafting personal surprises and engaging all the senses, this chapter has shown that romance can take many forms—each unique to the people involved.

Whether you're planning an intimate dinner, embracing shared vulnerability, or creating a budget-friendly day full of love, the common thread is your effort and intention. The most meaningful romantic moments are those that make your partner feel seen, valued, and cherished. These dates are more than just events—they are the building blocks of lasting intimacy.

As we move forward, we'll take the foundation of romance and add a spark of adventure. Next, you'll discover how to plan dates that push boundaries, explore new experiences, and inject excitement into your relationship. Together, let's continue creating memories that inspire and connect.

Adventurous Dates

Adventure has a way of breathing life into relationships. Stepping out of your comfort zone and into thrilling, unexpected situations creates moments that are as exhilarating as they are memorable. Adventurous dates are about embracing the excitement of the unknown together—whether it's conquering a rock-climbing wall, exploring a new city, or simply laughing through the twists and turns of a scavenger hunt. These shared experiences not only create stories to tell but also strengthen the bond through teamwork and trust.

The beauty of adventurous dates lies in their versatility. They can be as daring as skydiving or as playful as a round of mini-golf. What makes them special is the element of novelty—trying something new with your partner allows you both to see each other in a fresh light. Adventure challenges you to rely on one another, laugh through the unexpected, and celebrate small victories, making every moment feel like a mini triumph.

Whether you're adrenaline junkies or simply looking to break out of a routine, this section is packed with ideas to inspire your next thrilling escapade. From mystery-solving adventures to outdoor explorations, you'll find plenty of ways to inject excitement and spontaneity into your relationship. Let's explore how a little adventure can go a long way in deepening your connection.

Thrill-Seeking Activities

For couples looking to inject a dose of adrenaline into their relationship, thrill-seeking activities are the ultimate choice. These dates are all about stepping outside your comfort zones and experiencing the rush of excitement together. Whether it's tackling a daring adventure sport or simply trying something new, these moments of exhilaration create unforgettable memories and strengthen your bond through shared challenges.

Examples of Thrill-Seeking Activities

- **Zip-Lining**: Soar through the treetops and enjoy the thrill of speed while taking in breathtaking views.

- **Indoor Skydiving**: Experience the sensation of free-falling without the need to jump out of a plane.
- **Rock Climbing**: Work together to scale a climbing wall or natural rock face, building trust and teamwork.
- **Bungee Jumping**: Take a literal leap of faith and enjoy the adrenaline rush of a lifetime.

Thrill-seeking dates push you out of your daily routine and into exciting, unfamiliar territory. These activities trigger a release of adrenaline and endorphins, which can heighten feelings of connection and excitement. Additionally, working together to overcome challenges—whether it's climbing a rock wall or conquering a fear of heights—builds trust and reinforces your ability to rely on one another.

Imagine a day spent zip-lining through a lush forest, where each leap off the platform feels like a mini victory. The shared thrill of soaring through the air and cheering each other on creates a memory you'll both treasure.
Thrill-seeking activities like these are perfect for couples who crave adventure and want to deepen their connection through shared excitement.

Mystery and Exploration

There's a unique charm in dates that revolve around mystery and discovery. These experiences spark curiosity and encourage teamwork, making them perfect for couples who love solving puzzles, uncovering hidden gems, or simply exploring new surroundings together. Mystery and exploration-based dates are all about turning the ordinary into an adventure.

Examples of Mystery and Exploration Activities

- **Escape Rooms**: Work together to solve clues and escape within the time limit—a thrilling way to test your problem-solving skills.
- **Scavenger Hunts**: Plan a treasure hunt in your city or neighborhood, with each clue leading to the next exciting location.
- **Urban Exploration**: Discover hidden spots in your town, like quirky cafés, street art, or historic landmarks.
- **Geocaching**: Embark on a real-world treasure hunt using GPS to find hidden caches in parks or urban areas.

Mystery-based dates tap into our natural curiosity and sense of adventure. They create opportunities for collaboration and communication, as you work together to solve puzzles, follow clues, or navigate new environments. These shared challenges foster trust and teamwork, while the sense of discovery adds an element of excitement to the date.

Picture this: You and your partner are in an escape room, racing against the clock to uncover clues and unlock the final door. The laughter, high-fives, and sense of accomplishment you share when you succeed create a lasting memory. Mystery and exploration dates like these transform a simple outing into a dynamic experience that brings you closer.

Outdoor Adventures

For couples who love the great outdoors, adventure often means embracing nature and the challenges it offers. Outdoor adventures are perfect for those who want to escape the hustle and bustle of daily life and connect in a setting that inspires awe and tranquility. These dates provide opportunities for exploration, teamwork, and shared accomplishments.

Examples of Outdoor Adventures

- **Hiking**: Explore scenic trails that challenge your physical endurance and reward you with stunning views.
- **Kayaking**: Paddle along serene rivers or lakes, enjoying the calm of the water and the thrill of navigating together.
- **Camping**: Spend a night under the stars, complete with a campfire, marshmallows, and shared stories.
- **Biking Trails**: Ride through picturesque landscapes, from forests to mountain paths.

Outdoor adventures combine the physical benefits of activity with the emotional rewards of teamwork and connection. These experiences allow you to unplug from technology, focus on each other, and build lasting memories in beautiful surroundings. Overcoming physical challenges together, like reaching a mountain summit or navigating a tricky trail, strengthens your bond and fosters a sense of achievement.

Imagine kayaking on a serene lake as the sun sets, the only sounds being the splash of your paddles and the calls of distant birds. The tranquility and shared effort create a moment of pure connection. Outdoor adventures like these not only bring you closer but also provide stories you'll cherish for years to come.

Playful Competitions

Injecting a bit of friendly competition into your dates can create excitement, laughter, and plenty of shared memories. Playful competitions bring out your fun-loving sides, giving you a chance to bond while embracing your competitive streaks. Whether it's a game of mini-golf or a head-to-head go-kart race, these dates are perfect for couples who thrive on energy and lighthearted fun.

Examples of Playful Competitions
- **Laser Tag**: Team up or compete against each other in a fast-paced, adrenaline-filled game.
- **Go-Karting**: Race around the track and see who can take the top spot.
- **Mini-Golf**: Enjoy a casual, fun game with plenty of opportunities for jokes and banter.
- **Bowling**: A classic option that's both competitive and relaxed.

Competitive dates add a unique dynamic to your relationship, encouraging teamwork and shared laughter. They're an excellent way to break the ice or inject energy into your routine. The lighthearted nature of these activities ensures that the focus stays on having fun, not on winning. Plus, they create plenty of opportunities for playful teasing and camaraderie.

Picture this: You're at a mini-golf course, cheering each other on—or laughing at a particularly tricky shot. The mix of competition and fun keeps the mood light and engaging, while the shared experience strengthens your connection. Playful competitions like these turn ordinary dates into lively, memorable adventures.

Adrenaline and Novelty

For couples who crave excitement and love pushing boundaries, adrenaline-filled dates are the perfect choice. These experiences are designed to thrill, challenge, and create unforgettable memories. Whether it's soaring through the skies or testing your bravery on the ground, adrenaline and novelty-based dates inject a sense of adventure and excitement into your relationship.

Examples of Adrenaline and Novelty Activities
- **Hot Air Balloon Rides**: Enjoy breathtaking views while floating high above the ground—a perfect mix of thrill and serenity.
- **Bungee Jumping**: Take a literal leap of faith together and share the adrenaline rush of free-falling.
- **Skydiving**: For the truly daring, experience the ultimate thrill by jumping from a plane.
- **Amusement Parks**: Ride roller coasters and try attractions that get your hearts racing.
- **Zip-Lining**: Glide through the treetops at exhilarating speeds while enjoying scenic views.

Adrenaline-filled activities release endorphins and dopamine, creating a natural high that enhances feelings of connection and excitement. Sharing these experiences helps build trust and reliance on one another, especially when facing challenges together. The novelty of trying something new adds a fresh dynamic to your relationship, making each moment even more memorable.

Picture this: You and your partner are standing at the edge of a platform, ready to take your first bungee jump. The mix of anticipation and exhilaration brings you closer as you cheer each other on and share in the thrill. Adrenaline and novelty-based dates like these create stories you'll tell for years and forge a deeper bond through shared excitement.

Building Confidence Through Adventure

Adventure isn't just about excitement; it's also about growth. Dates that challenge you physically, mentally, or emotionally can be a powerful tool for building confidence—both individually and as a couple. By stepping out of your comfort zones together, you create opportunities to overcome fears, achieve new milestones, and celebrate victories big and small.

Examples of Confidence-Building Activities
- **Rock Climbing**: Tackle the challenge of scaling a climbing wall or a natural rock face, celebrating each other's progress along the way.
- **Obstacle Courses**: Sign up for a mud run or adventure race that requires teamwork and determination.
- **Surfing Lessons**: Learn a new skill together while enjoying the thrill of riding the waves.
- **Public Speaking Challenges**: Attend an open mic night where you both share a story or try improv comedy.

These types of dates foster a sense of accomplishment, boosting self-esteem and reinforcing mutual support. By tackling challenges side by side, you strengthen your bond and build trust in each other's capabilities. The skills and confidence gained through these activities often carry over into other aspects of your relationship and life.

Imagine completing a ropes course together, cheering each other on as you navigate the high elements. Each step builds confidence, not only in your own abilities but in your partnership. Confidence-building adventures like these turn challenges into shared triumphs, leaving you both feeling empowered and connected.

Adventurous dates add a spark of excitement to any relationship, offering opportunities to break free from the ordinary and embrace new experiences together. From adrenaline-filled activities to moments of playful competition, these outings challenge you to step out of your comfort zone and share in the thrill of discovery. They're about creating stories you'll tell for years and building a connection rooted in teamwork, trust, and shared triumphs.

What makes adventurous dates so special is their ability to bring out different sides of each partner—courage, creativity, and a sense of fun. Whether you're soaring through the sky on a zip-line or cracking puzzles in an escape room, these adventures are more than just exciting—they're moments that deepen your bond and remind you of the joy of exploring life together.

As you plan your next adventure, remember that the goal isn't just to chase thrills but to strengthen your relationship through shared experiences. Let each new activity bring you closer, building confidence in each other and creating memories that will last a lifetime. Next, we'll dive into dates that prove romance doesn't have to break the bank—low-budget ideas filled with creativity and care. Let's continue the journey!

Low-Budget Dates

Romance doesn't have to come with a hefty price tag. Some of the most meaningful and memorable dates are born out of creativity, thoughtfulness, and a willingness to embrace simplicity. Low-budget dates focus on connecting with your partner without the pressure of lavish spending. Instead, they highlight shared experiences and the joy of small, meaningful gestures. Whether you're cooking together at home, exploring free events in your community, or taking a walk under the stars, these dates prove that love thrives on effort, not expense.

What makes low-budget dates so special is their versatility—they can be tailored to fit any relationship stage or personal preference. These dates encourage couples to think outside the box, find beauty in the simple things, and create a bond through shared creativity. They remind us that it's the quality of the time spent together, not the money spent, that makes a date truly unforgettable.

In this section, we'll explore practical ideas for low-budget dates that are rich in connection and fun. From DIY movie nights to outdoor adventures, you'll find plenty of inspiration to plan meaningful moments that don't break the bank. Let's dive into how you can turn everyday activities into extraordinary memories.

DIY Experiences

Creating something together can be one of the most rewarding and intimate ways to spend time with your partner. DIY experiences aren't just budget-friendly; they also allow you to work as a team, unleash your creativity, and enjoy the satisfaction of building or crafting something meaningful. These dates are perfect for adding a personal touch to your time together.

Examples of DIY Experiences

- **Cooking Together**: Choose a recipe you've always wanted to try and create a homemade feast, complete with dessert.
- **Crafting Projects**: Create personalized items like

photo frames, scrapbooks, or holiday decorations.
- **Painting or Drawing**: Set up a mini art studio at home and let your inner artists shine.
- **DIY Home Improvement**: Tackle a small project like building a shelf or rearranging a room to give your space a fresh look.

DIY experiences encourage teamwork and communication while offering a creative outlet for both partners. These activities are not only cost-effective but also foster a sense of accomplishment and pride in what you've created together. They provide a unique way to bond while developing new skills or exploring shared interests.

Imagine baking a cake together for the first time—flour dusting the countertops, laughter filling the kitchen as you navigate the recipe. The result, whether perfect or slightly messy, becomes a symbol of the effort and fun you shared. DIY experiences like these prove that the process matters more than the outcome, making them ideal for couples looking to connect without spending much.

Nature-Based Activities

The great outdoors offers an abundance of opportunities for low-cost, high-quality dates. Nature-based activities are perfect for couples who want to unwind, explore, and connect in a setting that's both peaceful and inspiring. Whether it's a hike through a local trail or a picnic under the stars, these dates are a beautiful reminder of the simple joys that come with being surrounded by nature.

Examples of Nature-Based Activities

- **Picnics**: Pack a simple meal and enjoy it in a scenic park or by the water.

- **Hiking**: Explore local trails, taking in the sights and sounds of the outdoors.
- **Stargazing**: Bring a blanket, lie back, and marvel at the night sky together.
- **Beach Walks**: Stroll along the shoreline, collecting shells or simply enjoying the sound of the waves.

Nature has a calming effect, making it the perfect backdrop for meaningful conversations and quiet reflection. These activities encourage mindfulness and help you reconnect not just with each other but with the world around you. They're also a great way to stay active and enjoy fresh air without spending much.

Imagine setting up a picnic at your favorite park—complete with sandwiches, fruit, and a cozy blanket. As the sun sets and the air cools, you share stories, laughter, and a moment of stillness surrounded by nature. Dates like these show that the most meaningful moments don't require extravagant planning, just a little effort and a love for the simple things in life.

Community Events

Exploring your local community can uncover hidden gems and provide unique, low-cost date opportunities. Community events like free concerts, farmers' markets, and museum days are perfect for couples who want to engage with their surroundings while enjoying each other's company. These dates not only strengthen your connection but also support local culture and activities.

Examples of Community Events

- **Free Concerts**: Check out local listings for outdoor music events or performances.

- **Farmers' Markets**: Stroll through the stalls, sample fresh produce, and pick up ingredients for a meal.
- **Museum Days**: Take advantage of free or discounted admission days to explore art, history, or science exhibits.
- **Outdoor Festivals**: Enjoy seasonal celebrations like food festivals, art fairs, or cultural parades.

Community events provide a vibrant and engaging backdrop for your date, encouraging you to explore new experiences together. These activities are often free or low-cost, making them accessible to everyone. They also offer a chance to connect with your local area and discover shared interests.

Picture walking hand-in-hand through a lively farmers' market, stopping to sample fresh fruit and chat with vendors. The relaxed atmosphere, combined with the joy of discovering something new, makes for a memorable and meaningful outing. Community events like these prove that romance can be found in the simple act of exploring your surroundings together.

Game and Movie Nights

Sometimes, the best dates happen in the comfort of your own home. Game and movie nights are classic low-budget options that allow couples to unwind, have fun, and share laughter without stepping out the door. These dates are all about creating a cozy, personalized experience that feels special and intimate.

Examples of Game and Movie Nights

- **Board Games or Card Games**: Challenge each other to a game night with your favorite classics or discover new ones.

- **Video Games**: Team up or compete in co-op or multiplayer games for a fun and interactive evening.
- **Movie Marathons**: Pick a theme or series you both love and create a lineup for the night.
- **DIY Movie Night**: Set up a projector or create a cozy fort in the living room for a more cinematic experience.

These dates are not only budget-friendly but also incredibly versatile. They allow you to tailor the experience to your interests and mood, whether you're in for a competitive game session or a laid-back movie marathon. The relaxed environment encourages meaningful conversations and laughter, strengthening your bond in a stress-free setting.

Imagine spending the evening playing a nostalgic board game, complete with snacks and playful banter. Or picture yourselves watching a favorite movie, wrapped in blankets with homemade popcorn. Game and movie nights prove that sometimes, the simplest plans create the most memorable moments.

Volunteer Together

Few things are as fulfilling as giving back to the community, and doing so with your partner can make the experience even more meaningful. Volunteering together not only strengthens your bond but also provides an opportunity to connect over shared values and make a positive impact. These dates are perfect for couples who want to combine quality time with a sense of purpose.

Examples of Volunteer Activities

- **Animal Shelters**: Spend a day walking dogs, playing with cats, or helping with tasks at a local shelter.
- **Community Clean-Up**: Join efforts to clean up parks,

beaches, or other public spaces.
- **Soup Kitchens or Food Banks**: Assist in preparing and serving meals for those in need.
- **Charity Events**: Participate in fundraising walks, runs, or events for a cause you both support.

Volunteering creates a shared sense of purpose and accomplishment, allowing you to see your partner's compassionate and altruistic side. These activities encourage teamwork and can lead to meaningful conversations about the values and goals you share. Additionally, they offer a refreshing break from traditional date ideas while making a tangible difference in the community.

Imagine spending a morning planting trees in a community park, working side by side to leave a lasting impact. The shared effort, combined with the satisfaction of contributing to a good cause, creates a unique bonding experience. Volunteering together proves that love can thrive in the act of giving, enriching your relationship in ways that go beyond the ordinary.

Low-budget dates remind us that meaningful connections don't require extravagant spending. These experiences focus on creativity, shared effort, and the simple joy of spending time together. From creating something unique with DIY projects to exploring the great outdoors or giving back through volunteer work, each idea offers a chance to deepen your bond without breaking the bank.

The true value of these dates lies in their ability to bring couples closer, fostering laughter, conversation, and mutual appreciation. Whether you're picnicking in the park, enjoying a game night, or discovering hidden gems in your community, these moments prove that love thrives on thoughtfulness and effort—not expense.

As we look ahead, we will explore dates that blend romance with family inclusivity, showing how to create moments that strengthen not only your relationship but also your connections with loved ones. Let's continue this journey of discovery together.

Family-Inclusive Dates

Romance doesn't have to exist in isolation. For couples who share their lives with children, extended family, or close-knit groups of friends, family-inclusive dates offer a unique opportunity to blend love and connection. These dates allow you to strengthen your relationship while also creating meaningful memories with the people who matter most. Far from complicating your time together, involving loved ones can add depth and joy to your experiences.

Family-inclusive dates are perfect for celebrating milestones, deepening family bonds, or simply sharing the joy of being together. From cooking classes to game nights, these activities emphasize collaboration, fun, and shared laughter. By thoughtfully integrating family into your romantic plans, you create a sense of unity and foster a supportive environment where everyone feels valued.

In this section, we'll explore creative ideas for family-inclusive dates that cater to all ages and interests. Whether it's an outdoor hike, a group movie night, or a family-friendly workshop, you'll discover ways to balance romance with inclusivity. Let's dive into the art of blending love and family into unforgettable shared moments.

Group Cooking Classes

Few activities bring people together like preparing and sharing a meal. Group cooking classes are an excellent way to combine romance with family inclusivity, allowing everyone to bond over creativity, teamwork, and, of course, delicious food. Whether it's a guided class or a DIY cooking session at home, these dates are perfect for creating memories that everyone can savor.

Examples of Group Cooking Classes

- **Pasta-Making Night**: Learn how to roll dough, cut noodles, and create sauces as a team.
- **Sushi Rolling Workshop**: Dive into the art of sushi-making with interactive lessons for all ages.
- **Bake-Off Challenge**: Host a fun competition to see who can make the most creative or delicious baked treats.
- **Cultural Cuisine Exploration**: Pick a cuisine from a specific culture and cook a meal inspired by its traditional dishes.

Cooking together encourages collaboration, communication, and plenty of laughter. It's an interactive experience that gives everyone a role, from chopping vegetables to setting the table. These classes also allow you to celebrate each person's unique contributions, fostering a sense of togetherness. Plus, the shared reward of enjoying a delicious meal makes the effort worthwhile.

Picture this: You're gathered in the kitchen with your family, kneading dough for homemade pizza while your partner helps the kids arrange toppings. Laughter fills the room as someone accidentally sprinkles too much cheese, and the end result is a delicious, imperfectly perfect meal. Group cooking classes like these prove that the best dates are the ones that bring everyone closer together.

Family Game Nights

Nothing brings a family together quite like a night filled with laughter, friendly competition, and a shared sense of fun. Family game nights are an excellent way to create lasting memories while engaging everyone, from young children to grandparents. These evenings offer a relaxed environment where bonds are strengthened, and everyone can feel included.

Examples of Family Game Nights

- **Classic Board Games**: Dust off favorites like Monopoly, Scrabble, or Clue for timeless fun.
- **Card Games**: Play engaging games like Uno, Go Fish, or Rummy that cater to all ages.
- **Video Game Competitions**: Choose family-friendly multiplayer games like Mario Kart or Just Dance.
- **DIY Trivia Night**: Create trivia questions about family history, pop culture, or shared interests.

Game nights foster teamwork, problem-solving, and communication while encouraging laughter and playfulness. They provide a chance to disconnect from screens and daily stressors, creating a space for genuine connection. The inclusive nature of games ensures that everyone, regardless of age or skill level, can participate and contribute to the fun.

Imagine the entire family huddled around the coffee table, cheering and laughing as someone draws the winning card in Uno. The energy, excitement, and shared moments of triumph and humor make family game nights an unforgettable experience. These evenings show that sometimes, the simplest activities can create the most cherished memories.

Outdoor Adventures

Spending time outdoors offers a refreshing way to connect as a family while enjoying the beauty of nature. Outdoor adventures are perfect for creating shared memories, encouraging physical activity, and fostering a sense of exploration. These activities are accessible and enjoyable for family members of all ages, making them an ideal choice for inclusive dates.

Examples of Outdoor Adventures
- **Family Hikes**: Choose trails suitable for all ages and enjoy the sights, sounds, and fresh air together.
- **Beach Outings**: Spend the day building sandcastles, collecting seashells, or enjoying a picnic by the water.
- **Park Picnics**: Pack a basket of snacks, bring a frisbee or soccer ball, and enjoy quality time in the park.
- **Nature Scavenger Hunts**: Create a list of items to find, like specific leaves, rocks, or birds, and explore together.

Outdoor adventures provide a healthy mix of fun, relaxation, and discovery. They encourage families to step away from screens and engage with the world around them, offering opportunities for meaningful conversations and teamwork. The physical activity also boosts mood and energy levels, leaving everyone feeling refreshed.

Picture this: Your family embarks on a gentle hike through a forest, pausing to marvel at a waterfall and snap photos together. Along the way, laughter echoes as someone spots a squirrel or points out a unique plant. Outdoor adventures like these create a shared sense of wonder and connection, proving that nature is the perfect backdrop for family-inclusive dates.

Creative Workshops

Unleashing creativity as a family is not only fun but also a wonderful way to bond. Creative workshops allow everyone to explore their artistic sides, collaborate on projects, and take home a tangible memory of the experience. These dates are perfect for fostering teamwork and celebrating each person's unique contributions.

Examples of Creative Workshops

- **Painting Classes**: Attend a group painting session where everyone creates their own masterpiece.
- **Pottery Workshops**: Get hands-on with clay and create personalized bowls, mugs, or decorations.
- **DIY Craft Nights**: Host a crafting session at home with supplies for making holiday decorations, photo frames, or jewelry.
- **Cooking or Baking Workshops**: Combine creativity with delicious results by learning to make pastries, pasta, or desserts together.

Creative workshops provide a relaxed environment where family members can express themselves and collaborate on fun projects. These activities promote teamwork, patience, and a sense of accomplishment, as everyone contributes to the final creations. Plus, the tangible keepsakes serve as lasting reminders of the time spent together.

Imagine the joy of attending a pottery workshop where each family member molds their own creation. The laughter and stories shared during the process make the experience unforgettable, while the finished pieces become cherished keepsakes. Creative workshops like these bring out the best in everyone, turning simple moments into treasured memories.

Seasonal Celebrations

Seasonal activities provide the perfect opportunity to create family-inclusive dates that celebrate the time of year. From holiday traditions to seasonal outings, these dates are a great way to connect with loved ones while embracing the unique charm of each season. Whether it's carving pumpkins in the fall or decorating cookies in the winter, these activities make the most of festive moments.

Examples of Seasonal Celebrations

- **Pumpkin Carving**: Gather around to carve creative designs into pumpkins for Halloween.
- **Holiday Cookie Decorating**: Bake and decorate cookies as a family during the winter holidays.
- **Spring Flower Planting**: Welcome the warmer weather by planting flowers or starting a garden together.
- **Summer Beach Bonfires**: Enjoy a warm evening by the beach with s'mores, stories, and songs.

Seasonal activities provide a sense of tradition and anticipation, creating opportunities for meaningful bonding. They encourage families to engage with the time of year, making each moment feel special and unique. These activities also help create cherished traditions that can be looked forward to year after year.

Picture a winter evening spent decorating gingerbread houses with your family, laughing over frosting mishaps and sharing creative ideas. Or imagine a summer day at the beach, roasting marshmallows over a bonfire as the sun sets. Seasonal celebrations like these turn ordinary moments into cherished memories, bringing the whole family closer together.

Family-inclusive dates are a beautiful way to strengthen both romantic and familial bonds. These experiences remind us that love grows best when it's shared, creating moments of joy, laughter, and connection that everyone can cherish. From cooking meals together to celebrating seasonal traditions, each activity highlights the importance of togetherness.

The magic of family-inclusive dates lies in their ability to bring people closer, whether through teamwork, creativity, or simple shared fun. They foster communication, deepen relationships, and create lasting memories that go beyond the surface. By blending romance with inclusivity, these dates enrich not only your partnership but also your family as a whole.

As we move forward, we will explore how to maintain connections across distances and adapt to modern challenges. Let's continue this journey of meaningful and creative dating, discovering new ways to bring love and connection to the forefront of our lives.

Virtual and Long-Distance Dates

Love knows no boundaries, but physical distance can sometimes make it challenging to stay connected. Virtual and long-distance dates provide creative ways for couples to bridge the gap, fostering intimacy and shared experiences even when miles apart. Thanks to modern technology, meaningful connections are no longer confined to being in the same room. From virtual dinner dates to synchronized movie nights, these experiences bring a sense of closeness and excitement to long-distance relationships.

Virtual and long-distance dates are not just for couples separated by geography—they're also perfect for busy schedules or trying something unique from the comfort of home. These dates emphasize creativity, thoughtfulness, and the ability to adapt, proving that love thrives when we make the effort to connect. They provide an opportunity to deepen emotional bonds, share everyday moments, and even explore the world together through virtual means.

In this section, we'll explore a variety of virtual and long-distance date ideas that cater to different interests and preferences. Whether it's an online cooking class, a shared gaming session, or a virtual tour of a museum, these activities show that distance is no obstacle to love and creativity.

Synchronized Movie Nights

Synchronized movie nights are a classic yet deeply intimate way to connect, no matter the distance. The simple act of sharing a film together can foster a sense of togetherness that transcends physical boundaries. Choose a movie you both love or one neither of you has seen before for a fresh shared experience.

To make the evening special, consider setting up a video call alongside the streaming platform. React to funny moments, share commentary, and even pause to discuss your thoughts—just like you would if you were sitting on the same couch. For added ambiance, sync up on snacks and drinks, like making popcorn at the same time or enjoying a shared dessert remotely. Apps like Teleparty or Kast make the synchronization process effortless by aligning playback and enabling live chat.

This type of date is more than just entertainment; it's a way to nurture connection, laughter, and shared joy. Whether you're enjoying a rom-com, an action thriller, or a nostalgic classic, synchronized movie nights prove that distance is no obstacle to creating cherished memories.

Online Gaming Sessions

Online gaming sessions are an engaging way to connect, offering opportunities for teamwork, friendly competition, and shared laughter. Games bring a sense of playfulness and collaboration that can strengthen your bond, no matter the distance.

Start by choosing multiplayer games that align with your interests and dynamic as a couple. For a cooperative experience, explore puzzle games or role-playing adventures where teamwork is essential. If you're both competitive, dive into trivia quizzes or strategy games that allow you to challenge each other. Games like "Among Us," "Overcooked," or classic card games available online can create a blend of fun and connection.

To make the session special, set up a voice or video call alongside the gameplay. Share real-time reactions, strategize together, or laugh about unexpected moments during the game. For added excitement, you could turn the gaming session into a themed night—like wearing costumes related to the game or preparing snacks inspired by the theme.

Online gaming isn't just about the activity itself; it's about creating moments of joy, discovery, and camaraderie. Whether you're solving a puzzle together, racing to the finish line, or competing for the top score, these sessions are an excellent way to keep your connection strong while having a blast.

Virtual Cooking or Crafting Classes

Virtual cooking or crafting classes are a delightful way to bond while creating something meaningful together. These experiences combine creativity, teamwork, and the joy of shared accomplishment, all from the comfort of your own spaces.

Start by selecting a class that aligns with your interests. If you're food enthusiasts, try an online cooking class where you can learn to make a new dish together, from homemade pasta to international cuisines. If you prefer hands-on crafting, explore workshops for pottery, painting, or DIY projects like candle-making or personalized keepsakes. Websites like MasterClass, Skillshare, or YouTube offer a wide variety of classes to suit every interest and skill level.

To make the experience even more engaging, set up your video call in a way that feels interactive and fun. Share progress updates, compare your creations, and exchange tips as you go. Don't worry about perfection—the focus is on enjoying the process and the laughter that comes with it. For added fun, consider surprising your partner with a theme, like a romantic dinner recipe or seasonal craft.

The magic of virtual cooking or crafting classes lies in the effort you put into learning and creating something together. Whether it's a delicious meal to share virtually or a handmade item to keep, these experiences bring a sense of closeness, creativity, and accomplishment that transcends physical distance.

Exploring Virtual Worlds

Exploring virtual worlds is an exciting way to connect while discovering new environments and experiences together. From immersive virtual reality events to online tours of museums and scenic locations, these adventures bring the thrill of exploration to your screen.

Start by selecting an activity that matches your shared interests. For art enthusiasts, virtual museum tours like those offered by the Louvre or the Smithsonian allow you to marvel at world-class exhibits. Music lovers can attend VR concerts or live-streamed performances, while adventurers can explore scenic locations through 360-degree virtual tours of national parks, landmarks, or even outer space. Platforms like Google Arts & Culture or dedicated VR apps make these experiences accessible.

To enhance the experience, schedule time to explore together via a video call. Share your thoughts, point out intriguing details, and discuss what you're seeing in real time. For couples with VR headsets, dive into interactive environments, such as multiplayer VR games or themed experiences like virtual escape rooms or fantasy worlds.

These virtual journeys are more than just digital experiences—they're opportunities to learn, laugh, and bond. Whether you're gazing at famous artwork, walking through ancient ruins, or attending a live event, exploring virtual worlds showcases how creativity and technology can keep your connection alive and thriving.

Custom Online Experiences

Custom online experiences are a deeply personal way to connect and celebrate your unique bond, no matter the distance. These tailor-made dates allow you to design creative and meaningful moments that reflect your shared interests and love story.

Start by brainstorming activities that resonate with your relationship. For a romantic touch, write letters or poems for each other and read them aloud during a video call. If music brings you closer, curate a playlist of songs that hold special meaning and listen together, sharing memories tied to each track. For a collaborative project, consider creating a digital photo album or scrapbook filled with shared moments and captions.

To make the experience extra special, personalize the details. For example, if you're celebrating a milestone, create a themed night—like recreating your first date virtually or planning a "future goals" session where you dream together about your next adventures. Use digital tools like Canva for creative designs or online collaboration platforms for building projects together.

Custom online experiences highlight the thoughtfulness and effort you bring to the relationship. These dates aren't just about spending time together—they're about celebrating the little things that make your connection unique. Whether you're crafting a playlist, working on a creative project, or simply sharing heartfelt words, these moments will leave a lasting impression.

Virtual and long-distance dates remind us that love transcends physical boundaries. In a world where distance can sometimes feel like a barrier, these creative and thoughtful experiences show how connection thrives on effort and imagination. Whether you're sharing laughs during a synchronized movie night, collaborating on a craft project, or exploring virtual worlds together, these moments bring intimacy and joy to your relationship, no matter the miles between you.

The beauty of these dates lies in their adaptability and personal touch. They allow you to celebrate your bond in meaningful ways, from embracing playful gaming sessions to curating deeply personal experiences like writing letters or sharing playlists. By focusing on connection and creativity, you can turn everyday activities into cherished memories that strengthen your relationship.

As we conclude this section, take inspiration from the possibilities and challenges of virtual dating. Let these ideas spark your imagination and encourage you to craft unique experiences that bring you closer together. Next, we'll explore how romance can flourish when shared with family, creating moments that unite your loved ones while deepening your relationship. Let's continue the journey of meaningful connection and creative dating.

Self-Care and Wellness Dates:

Nurturing Love Through Wellness

In today's fast-paced world, finding moments to slow down and focus on well-being is essential—for both individuals and couples. Self-care and wellness dates are a beautiful way to prioritize health, mindfulness, and connection. These dates aren't just about relaxation; they're about creating a shared space to recharge, grow closer, and nurture your relationship.

The beauty of self-care dates lies in their versatility. Whether you're unwinding with a spa night at home, embracing the outdoors through yoga, or exploring mindfulness practices together, these experiences foster both physical and emotional intimacy. They encourage you to support each other's well-being while creating meaningful memories rooted in care and connection.

In this section, we'll explore a variety of self-care and wellness date ideas that cater to different preferences and lifestyles. From tranquil evenings focused on relaxation to active outings that energize and inspire, these dates are designed to help you and your partner feel your best—together. Let's dive into the art of wellness and discover how self-care can deepen your bond while enriching your life.

Couples' Yoga or Meditation

Yoga and meditation are powerful tools for cultivating relaxation, balance, and emotional connection, making them an ideal choice for self-care dates. Practicing these mindfulness activities together not only benefits your individual well-being but also strengthens your bond by fostering presence and harmony in your relationship.

Start by selecting a practice that suits your comfort level and goals. Beginners might explore simple yoga routines or guided meditations available on apps like Calm or YouTube. For a deeper experience, consider joining a local yoga studio or attending a virtual class tailored for couples. You can even create a peaceful space at home with soft lighting, relaxing music, and mats placed side by side.

As you move through poses or focus on your breath, encourage open communication and mutual support. Yoga poses designed for pairs, such as partner stretches or balancing poses, add a playful and intimate element to your practice. Meditation sessions can be enhanced by sharing intentions or reflecting on your experiences afterward.

The beauty of couples' yoga or meditation lies in its ability to ground you both in the present moment, helping you to feel more connected and at peace. Whether you're holding a pose together or simply sharing a moment of stillness, these practices remind you to prioritize your well-being and the strength of your partnership.

Spa Nights at Home

Transform your home into a serene retreat with a DIY spa night, creating the perfect blend of relaxation, rejuvenation, and romance. This self-care date allows you to unwind and connect in a tranquil environment, free from distractions.

Start by setting the mood with soft lighting, candles, and calming music. Gather essentials like plush towels, face masks, massage oils, and soothing bath products. Consider adding a touch of luxury with aromatherapy diffusers or fresh flowers to elevate the atmosphere.

Your spa night can include a variety of activities tailored to your preferences. Begin with a warm bubble bath or foot soak, followed by applying face masks or exfoliating scrubs. Take turns giving each other massages, using techniques you can easily learn from online tutorials. For an extra treat, prepare refreshing drinks like herbal tea, fruit-infused water, or even a glass of wine to sip between treatments.

The beauty of a spa night at home lies in its intimacy and simplicity. These moments of relaxation encourage deeper connection, as you focus on nurturing each other's well-being. Whether you're indulging in a full pampering session or simply enjoying quiet time together, spa nights remind you to slow down, unwind, and savor the joy of being present with one another.

Outdoor Wellness Activities

Nature has a unique way of rejuvenating the mind, body, and spirit, making outdoor wellness activities a perfect choice for couples looking to combine self-care with quality time. These experiences provide an opportunity to disconnect from daily stresses, reconnect with each other, and soak in the healing power of the outdoors.

Start by exploring activities that align with your interests and fitness levels. A gentle hike through scenic trails can offer moments of awe and tranquility, while forest bathing—a practice of immersing yourself in the sights and sounds of nature—can promote mindfulness and relaxation. Riverside meditations or yoga sessions on a beach provide a calming backdrop for grounding and balance.

Enhance the experience by incorporating small touches that make the outing memorable. Pack a picnic with healthy snacks, bring a journal to jot down reflections, or create a shared playlist to accompany your walk. Engaging your senses with the sights, sounds, and scents of nature can deepen your connection and amplify the restorative benefits.

The beauty of outdoor wellness activities lies in their ability to nurture both your relationship and your overall well-being. Whether you're strolling through a lush park, meditating under a canopy of trees, or practicing yoga at sunrise, these moments remind you of the importance of slowing down and savoring life's simple pleasures—together.

Fitness Challenges for Two

Engaging in fitness challenges as a couple is a dynamic way to promote health, teamwork, and mutual motivation. These activities not only help you stay active but also strengthen your bond as you support each other in reaching shared goals.

Start by choosing a challenge that excites both of you. It could be training for a charity run, committing to a daily yoga practice, or following a workout plan that builds strength and endurance. If you prefer something more adventurous, try activities like cycling long distances, mastering a rock-climbing wall, or even competing in a friendly tennis match.

To make the experience more meaningful, set achievable milestones and celebrate your progress along the way. Track your workouts, share words of encouragement, and reward yourselves with small treats for hitting key goals—like a smoothie date after a tough session or a relaxing stretch together. Apps like Strava or MyFitnessPal can help you monitor progress and stay on track.

The key to fitness challenges for two is finding joy in the process. Whether you're cheering each other on during a run, laughing through a difficult yoga pose, or competing for the fastest lap on the track, these moments of effort and accomplishment bring you closer. Fitness challenges aren't just about physical health—they're about building trust, camaraderie, and a sense of shared victory in your journey toward well-being.

Healthy Cooking Adventures

Healthy cooking adventures offer the perfect mix of creativity, fun, and nourishment. Preparing nutritious meals together allows you to explore new flavors, bond over shared tasks, and prioritize your well-being as a couple.

Start by choosing a recipe that excites both of you. Whether it's a plant-based dish, a protein-packed entrée, or a vibrant smoothie bowl, focus on options that align with your health goals and dietary preferences. To make the experience even more interactive, visit a local farmers' market to pick out fresh ingredients together.

Transform your kitchen into a space for culinary exploration. Divide tasks like chopping, seasoning, or plating to keep things collaborative, and don't shy away from experimenting with spices or techniques. For added fun, turn the cooking session into a themed evening—like an Italian night with homemade pasta or a tropical twist featuring fruity mocktails and island-inspired dishes.

Healthy cooking adventures are more than just about the food. They encourage teamwork, laughter, and the satisfaction of creating something meaningful together. By focusing on nourishing both your bodies and your relationship, these moments leave you feeling energized and connected. And the best part? You get to enjoy the delicious fruits of your labor as a reward for your shared efforts.

Wellness Retreats or Workshops

Wellness retreats or workshops offer couples an immersive experience to focus on health, relaxation, and growth. These escapes provide a break from the routine and create opportunities for deeper connection through shared learning and rejuvenation.

Explore retreats or workshops that align with your shared interests. Options include yoga and mindfulness retreats, fitness boot camps, or holistic health programs that cover topics like nutrition, stress management, or aromatherapy. Many retreats are held in serene locations like mountain lodges, seaside resorts, or wellness centers, enhancing the restorative atmosphere.

If time or budget is a concern, consider one-day workshops or virtual sessions. These allow you to participate in guided activities such as sound baths, meditation exercises, or nutrition classes without committing to an extended stay.

Look for events in your area or online platforms offering interactive experiences tailored to couples.

The beauty of wellness retreats and workshops lies in their transformative potential. They help you not only recharge physically and emotionally but also gain valuable tools for maintaining a healthy and fulfilling relationship. Whether you're embracing a weekend getaway or diving into a virtual workshop, these experiences provide a fresh perspective and lasting benefits for both your partnership and individual well-being.

Self-care and wellness dates remind us that nurturing a relationship starts with nurturing ourselves. By prioritizing health, mindfulness, and relaxation, these moments allow couples to recharge individually and grow stronger together. Whether it's the calm of a yoga session, the fun of a fitness challenge, or the creativity of healthy cooking adventures, wellness dates bring balance and harmony to your connection.

The true beauty of self-care dates lies in their ability to align your well-being with your partnership. These experiences foster trust, communication, and mutual support, creating a foundation for long-term happiness. They also remind us of the importance of slowing down and savoring life's simple joys, from a peaceful outdoor hike to a cozy spa night at home.

As we move forward, take inspiration from the practices and ideas shared in this chapter. Let them guide you in making wellness a regular part of your relationship, ensuring that both your love and your health continue to flourish. In the next section, we'll explore how dates rooted in cultural discovery can inspire and enrich your bond, bringing new dimensions of connection to your shared journey.

Culturally Immersive Dates

Every culture has its own stories, flavors, and traditions that connect us to the larger human experience. Culturally immersive dates offer couples a unique opportunity to explore these rich tapestries together, fostering curiosity, understanding, and a shared sense of adventure. Whether you're tasting cuisines from around the world, attending cultural festivals, or learning a new dance style, these experiences create meaningful memories while deepening your connection.

The beauty of culturally immersive dates lies in their ability to inspire. They encourage couples to step outside their comfort zones, embrace diversity, and discover new dimensions of their relationship. These moments are not just about entertainment—they're about growth, appreciation, and the joy of shared discovery.

In this section, we'll explore creative ways to infuse your dates with cultural exploration. From cooking classes to global film nights, these ideas will help you bring the world to your relationship, one experience at a time.

Food Festivals and Culinary Experiences

Food has a unique way of connecting people to culture, history, and each other. Attending food festivals or engaging in culinary experiences allows couples to savor the flavors of the world while creating meaningful memories. These dates are perfect for adventurers with curious palates and a love for discovering new tastes.

Start by researching local or regional food festivals that highlight specific cuisines or cultural traditions. Events like Greek food fairs, Latin American street markets, or Asian night bazaars offer an immersive experience with authentic dishes, live music, and vibrant atmospheres. If a festival isn't an option, consider signing up for a cooking class that teaches you to prepare traditional recipes, such as sushi, pasta, or curries.

For a more intimate experience, bring the festival home. Plan a themed cooking night where you explore a specific cuisine together. Gather ingredients, follow a recipe, and enjoy the satisfaction of creating an authentic meal as a team. Add ambiance with music, decorations, or even learning a few cultural facts about the cuisine you're exploring.

Food festivals and culinary experiences are more than just about eating—they're about sharing the stories, traditions, and creativity that shape each dish. Whether you're sampling exotic street food or perfecting a family recipe, these dates deepen your bond through the joy of discovery and the universal language of flavor.

Dance and Music Workshops

Dance and music are universal expressions of culture and emotion, making them a vibrant and engaging way to connect with each other and the world around you. Participating in dance and music workshops as a couple allows you to step into new rhythms, discover shared joy, and embrace the beauty of diverse traditions.

Start by choosing a workshop that intrigues you both. If you're drawn to high-energy activities, try salsa, African drumming, or swing dance lessons. For something more graceful, consider a class in traditional waltz, tango, or flamenco. Many communities and cultural organizations offer beginner-friendly workshops where you can learn the basics in a welcoming environment.

To enhance the experience, immerse yourselves in the music and movements. Pay attention to the stories and traditions behind the art form, and let the rhythm guide you. If in-person workshops aren't an option, online platforms provide accessible and interactive tutorials for various dance and music styles.

The magic of dance and music workshops lies in their ability to bring couples closer. The physical connection of dance, combined with the shared energy of music, creates an atmosphere of playfulness and intimacy. Whether you're mastering steps together or laughing through a few missteps, these experiences celebrate creativity, collaboration, and the universal joy of movement and sound.

Global Movie Nights

Movies are windows into the stories, traditions, and emotions of cultures worldwide. Hosting a global movie night is an inspiring way to immerse yourselves in another part of the world, sparking curiosity, meaningful conversations, and a deeper understanding of diverse perspectives.

Start by choosing a film from a culture or country you're curious about. Platforms like Criterion Channel, Netflix, or local libraries often feature international films, ranging from romantic dramas to thrilling adventures. Consider exploring classic works from legendary filmmakers such as Akira Kurosawa, Satyajit Ray, or Ingmar Bergman, or diving into contemporary favorites like South Korean thrillers or French romantic comedies.

To make the night more immersive, create an atmosphere that complements the film's setting. Prepare snacks or drinks inspired by the culture, like dim sum for a Chinese film or crepes for a French movie. After the movie, take time to discuss its themes, characters, and cultural elements. Reflect on how the film portrays universal experiences like love, loss, or courage while revealing unique cultural nuances.

Global movie nights are more than just entertainment—they're an opportunity to travel the world from your couch, expanding your horizons as a couple. These evenings foster a sense of connection, not only to each other but also to the global community, reminding you of the beauty and complexity of shared human experiences.

Museum and Art Exhibitions

Museums and art exhibitions are portals into the history, creativity, and stories of cultures around the world. Visiting these spaces as a couple is a thoughtful and enriching way to connect while deepening your appreciation for the arts, heritage, and shared human experiences.

Begin by exploring local or regional museums that feature exhibits on different cultures, histories, or art movements. Look for special exhibitions that highlight traditional artifacts, contemporary art, or themes like ancient civilizations or modern global issues. If you're unable to visit in person, many museums offer virtual tours or online galleries, allowing you to explore their collections from anywhere.

To enhance the experience, approach your visit with curiosity and engagement. Discuss your favorite pieces, the emotions they evoke, and the stories they tell. For added fun, create a mini scavenger hunt—challenge each other to find certain items or themes within the exhibit. If the museum allows, take notes or photos to reflect on later.

Museum and art exhibition dates are about more than just viewing displays—they're about discovering new perspectives and sharing moments of awe and inspiration. Whether you're admiring ancient artifacts or exploring bold modern art, these experiences spark meaningful conversations and strengthen your bond through a shared appreciation of culture and creativity.

Cultural Celebrations and Festivals

Cultural celebrations and festivals offer a lively and immersive way to experience the traditions, music, and flavors of different communities. Attending these events as a couple allows you to embrace diversity, share joyful moments, and create memories steeped in vibrant cultural expressions.

Start by researching festivals in your area or planning a trip to a renowned cultural celebration. Events like Lunar New Year, Diwali, Oktoberfest, or Carnival showcase unique customs, performances, and culinary delights. Many cities also host multicultural festivals that bring together a variety of traditions in one place, offering a broad array of experiences.

To make the most of the celebration, immerse yourselves in the event's activities. Participate in traditional dances, sample authentic cuisine, or join workshops that teach you about the festival's history and significance. Capture the experience with photos or videos to reflect on later and deepen your appreciation for the culture.

The beauty of cultural celebrations and festivals lies in their ability to bring people together. These events are not just about observing—they're about participating in the joy and spirit of a community. Whether you're dancing under colorful lights, tasting new dishes, or simply marveling at the traditions, these dates create lasting memories while broadening your understanding of the world.

Language and Craft Classes

Learning a new language or engaging in traditional crafts as a couple is a creative and enriching way to explore a culture together. These experiences not only introduce you to the beauty of another heritage but also encourage teamwork, patience, and shared growth.

Start by selecting an activity that aligns with your interests. If you're intrigued by language, take an introductory class or follow an app like Duolingo or Babbel to learn basic phrases. Practice speaking with each other, and add a fun twist by role-playing scenarios, such as ordering food at a café or planning a trip. If crafts appeal to you, explore workshops that teach skills like pottery, weaving, calligraphy, or even traditional cooking techniques.

Enhance the experience by incorporating cultural context. For instance, while learning a language, explore its cultural idioms or expressions, and while crafting, learn about the history and significance of the art form. Many communities and online platforms offer classes that combine practical learning with storytelling, making the experience more immersive.

The beauty of language and craft classes lies in their ability to connect you to a culture while fostering a sense of achievement. Whether you're mastering the basics of a new language or creating a beautiful piece of art, these activities strengthen your bond and leave you with skills and memories that you'll treasure for years to come.

Culturally immersive dates remind us of the beauty, diversity, and interconnectedness of the world we share. By exploring traditions, cuisines, arts, and stories from different cultures, you and your partner can deepen your appreciation for each other and the broader human experience. These dates are more than activities—they're opportunities to grow, learn, and celebrate life together.

The magic of cultural exploration lies in its ability to inspire curiosity and connection. Whether you're savoring dishes at a food festival, learning a traditional dance, or marveling at an art exhibit, these shared moments create lasting memories rooted in discovery and joy. They also foster empathy and understanding, enriching your relationship with new perspectives.

As we conclude this section, let the spirit of cultural immersion guide your future adventures. Continue to embrace the world's richness and let it strengthen your bond, one experience at a time. Next, we'll turn our attention to the magic of seasonal and holiday-inspired dates, exploring how the rhythm of the year can bring unique opportunities for love and connection.

Seasonal and Holiday-Inspired Dates

The changing seasons and special holidays provide a natural backdrop for romance, bringing opportunities to create magical and memorable moments. Seasonal and holiday-inspired dates celebrate the beauty of the world around us, while also offering a chance to embrace traditions, enjoy festivities, and savor the unique charm of each time of year. Whether it's a cozy winter evening, a festive holiday outing, or a vibrant summer adventure, these dates capture the essence of love in every season.

The magic of seasonal and holiday dates lies in their versatility. From intimate gatherings to spirited celebrations, they allow couples to bond over shared experiences while embracing the rhythms of the year. In this section, we'll explore a variety of creative ideas that bring the joy of the seasons and holidays into your relationship, helping you craft moments of connection, warmth, and fun.

Winter Wonderland Advent♦ures

Winter's frosty charm provides the perfect backdrop for cozy, romantic, and playful dates. From snowy escapades to warm indoor activities, winter wonderland adventures offer couples the chance to create magical memories while embracing the season's unique beauty.

Start by planning outdoor activities that make the most of the snowy weather. Ice skating at a local rink, sledding down a hill, or building snowmen together are playful ways to bond while enjoying the crisp winter air. If you're feeling adventurous, consider trying snowshoeing, skiing, or a horse-drawn sleigh ride for a truly unforgettable experience.

After the outdoor fun, transition to a warm and intimate setting. Wrap up the day with steaming mugs of hot cocoa or mulled cider, cuddled under blankets by the fire. Watch a holiday movie, bake cookies together, or spend the evening decorating your space with twinkling lights to capture the festive spirit.

Winter wonderland adventures combine the thrill of outdoor activities with the intimacy of cozy evenings. Whether you're laughing through a snowball fight or sharing a quiet moment by the fire, these dates celebrate the season's magic and bring you closer through shared joy and warmth.

Springtime Blooms and Picnics

Spring is a season of renewal and beauty, offering couples a vibrant setting to reconnect and celebrate life's simple pleasures. With blooming flowers, warming weather, and longer days, it's the perfect time to plan dates that embrace the season's charm.

Start by exploring botanical gardens, cherry blossom festivals, or tulip fields in your area. Wandering through a garden filled with colorful blooms is not only visually stunning but also provides a peaceful atmosphere for conversation and reflection. For a touch of adventure, look for walking trails that feature wildflowers or scenic views.

A picnic is another quintessential springtime activity. Pack a basket with your favorite foods, a cozy blanket, and maybe even a bottle of wine or sparkling water. Choose a picturesque location—like a park, a riverside spot, or a meadow—to spread out and enjoy the fresh air. Enhance the experience with small touches, like a bouquet of flowers or a playlist of soft tunes to set the mood.

Springtime dates are about celebrating nature's beauty and the energy of renewal. Whether you're admiring vibrant blossoms or sharing a meal under the sun, these moments offer a chance to pause, connect, and revel in the joy of the season.

Summer Nights and Outdoor Fun

Summer is a season of warmth, adventure, and endless possibilities for romantic and playful dates. From starlit evenings to sun-soaked adventures, summer nights and outdoor fun capture the magic of this vibrant season while deepening your connection.

Plan activities that make the most of the long days and balmy nights. Stargazing is a classic yet enchanting option—find a quiet spot away from city lights, bring a blanket, and admire the cosmos together. For an active twist, enjoy a sunset hike that ends with a scenic view. Beach outings, complete with sandcastle building or a moonlit walk along the shore, add a touch of relaxation and romance.

Summer is also the perfect time for outdoor events. Attend an open-air concert, a local food festival, or a movie night under the stars. If you prefer a more intimate setting, host a backyard barbecue for two, complete with homemade treats and your favorite music. For a playful touch, set up lawn games like badminton or cornhole to bring out your competitive side.

The beauty of summer lies in its energy and spontaneity. Whether you're savoring a warm evening by the water or dancing at a lively outdoor event, these dates celebrate the season's spirit and create lasting memories of joy, laughter, and love.

Autumn Fairs and Festivities

Autumn's crisp air, vibrant foliage, and festive traditions make it a season rich with romantic and nostalgic date opportunities. From cozy outings to playful adventures, autumn fairs and festivities bring warmth and joy to your relationship.

Start by visiting local orchards or pumpkin patches, where you can pick apples, choose the perfect pumpkin, or enjoy hayrides through scenic farmland. These activities are playful and interactive, offering plenty of opportunities for laughter and connection. For couples who love a little thrill, explore a corn maze or brave a haunted house together—it's a perfect excuse to stay close.

Local fall fairs are another hallmark of the season. Stroll hand-in-hand through colorful booths, sample seasonal treats like caramel apples or pumpkin spice goodies, and try your luck at classic carnival games. Don't forget to take a spin on the Ferris wheel for a picturesque view of the autumn landscape.

End the day with an autumn-inspired activity at home. Carve jack-o-lanterns together, bake a pie using your freshly picked apples, or snuggle up for a movie night featuring classic fall favorites. These quiet moments add a cozy touch to the day's adventures.

Autumn dates are all about savoring the season's charm and embracing its traditions. Whether you're wandering through a fair or sharing a pumpkin pie, these experiences bring a sense of warmth and togetherness that reflects the heart of the season.

Holiday Traditions and Celebrations

The holiday season is a time of warmth, magic, and cherished traditions, making it perfect for creating meaningful and memorable dates. Whether you're embracing longstanding customs or crafting new ones together, holiday celebrations bring joy and connection to your relationship.

Begin by diving into activities that reflect your favorite holiday traditions. Decorate a Christmas tree with ornaments that tell a story, light a menorah and exchange thoughtful gifts, or bake cookies using recipes passed down through generations. These simple yet heartfelt moments capture the spirit of the season while strengthening your bond.

For a more festive outing, explore holiday markets, attend local parades, or go ice skating at a holiday-themed rink. Look for community events like caroling, tree-lighting ceremonies, or seasonal plays to immerse yourselves in the festive atmosphere. If you're feeling adventurous, plan a trip to a winter wonderland destination, complete with snowy landscapes and holiday décor.

Make your celebrations unique by adding personal touches. Create a custom holiday playlist, craft handmade gifts for each other, or host a cozy themed dinner with favorite seasonal dishes. The effort and creativity you bring to these traditions will make them even more special.

Holiday traditions and celebrations are about more than just the activities—they're about the love and connection you share while embracing the season's magic. Whether you're sipping hot cocoa by the fire or strolling through a holiday market, these dates create cherished memories that last well beyond the season.

Seasonal DIY Projects

Seasonal DIY projects are a creative and intimate way to embrace the charm of each season while spending quality time together. From crafting decorations to making thoughtful gifts, these hands-on activities add a personal touch to your celebrations and deepen your bond as a couple.

Start by choosing a project that reflects the season. In the winter, try creating homemade ornaments, designing holiday cards, or knitting scarves to keep warm. Spring invites opportunities for planting flowers, building birdhouses, or making floral wreaths. Summer offers outdoor DIY projects like painting garden pots, crafting picnic blankets, or building a small firepit for cozy evenings. Autumn is perfect for carving pumpkins, creating harvest centerpieces, or making fall-scented candles.

To make the experience more memorable, set up a comfortable workspace with everything you need—craft supplies, snacks, and perhaps some background music to set the mood. Work as a team or create individual projects to showcase your unique styles, then admire the results together.

DIY projects are more than just creative activities—they're moments of collaboration, laughter, and shared achievement. These projects not only add a personal touch to your seasonal celebrations but also serve as lasting reminders of the time you've spent together. Whether you're decorating for the holidays or crafting something special for your home, seasonal DIY projects make the magic of each season even more meaningful.

Seasonal and holiday-inspired dates remind us to embrace the beauty and rhythm of the year, finding joy in every moment and memory we create. Whether it's the crisp excitement of autumn fairs, the cozy magic of winter evenings, or the vibrant energy of summer nights, these experiences celebrate the unique charm each season brings to our lives and relationships.

The true magic of these dates lies in their ability to blend tradition, creativity, and love. They encourage us to savor life's little joys—decorating a holiday tree, picnicking under spring blooms, or laughing through a corn maze—and to share those moments with the ones who matter most. These dates are not just about activities; they're about connection, celebration, and the beauty of being present with each other.

As we move forward, let the spirit of the seasons inspire your journey. In the next chapter, we'll explore adventurous and thrill-seeking dates, diving into experiences that ignite excitement, courage, and a sense of discovery. Together, we'll continue crafting moments that bring joy and connection to every aspect of your relationship.

The Psychology of Dating and Connection

Love is not just a chance encounter or the product of fate—it's a beautifully intricate dance of emotions, shared moments, and subconscious connections that grow stronger over time. At its core, love is not something we stumble into by accident; it's something we cultivate and nurture through intentional action. The way we connect with someone on a date often feels like magic, but beneath that sense of wonder lies a blend of psychological and emotional dynamics. Understanding these forces is essential to unlocking deeper connection and intimacy.

At the heart of every successful date is a profound awareness of what draws two people closer together. Whether it's the first spark of attraction or the steady, deliberate deepening of a bond over time, certain elements can make one date unforgettable while another fades into obscurity. The secret lies in a delicate interplay of chemistry, emotional bonding, and the ability to craft meaningful, lasting memories. These aren't abstract ideas; they are the building blocks of human connection, present in every glance, conversation, and shared experience.

When we think about the dates that stand out in our lives, they often aren't the ones with the fanciest settings or the grandest gestures. Instead, they are the moments that feel deeply personal, when connection takes center stage. It might be the way your partner leaned in to share an inside joke, their laughter filling the air like music, or the quiet comfort of walking hand in hand by the lake, saying little but feeling everything. These experiences are not random; they are carefully shaped by a complex mix of shared vulnerability, emotional resonance, and the natural rhythm of human connection.

The most memorable dates often arise from simple, thoughtful moments where you feel truly seen and heard. For example, a spontaneous picnic in the park, where mismatched sandwiches and a wrinkled blanket are elevated by the intimacy of the moment, can mean far more than a meal in an extravagant restaurant. These instances reveal the key to meaningful dating: it's not about perfection, but about presence. Understanding this intricate dance of connection is the foundation for creating deeper intimacy in your relationship.

Humans are inherently social creatures, driven to seek out and strengthen bonds with others. This innate need for connection is amplified through shared experiences, which act as powerful catalysts for emotional closeness. When two people come together to share an activity—whether it's tackling a challenging hike or attempting to paint a picture together—they transcend the boundaries of individual identity and begin to form a team. These moments of collaboration and discovery create a sense of "us" that replaces "me."

Shared activities provide a platform for mutual support, encouragement, and even laughter. Imagine two people building a bookshelf together. It's not just the finished product that matters; it's the process of figuring it out, laughing at mistakes, and high-fiving when the last screw is in place. These moments foster a sense of partnership, strengthening trust and deepening emotional intimacy.

Activities that require collaboration—whether playful or practical—are opportunities to build the kind of bond that feels lasting and genuine.

This phenomenon is not just a poetic notion; it's rooted in biology. When we engage in shared activities, our brains release dopamine, the hormone responsible for feelings of pleasure and reward, and oxytocin, often called the "bonding hormone." These neurochemicals don't just make us feel happy in the moment; they also strengthen the neural pathways that tie those feelings to the person we're sharing them with. Studies show that couples who participate in novel or challenging activities report higher levels of relationship satisfaction, as these experiences create lasting memories and deepen their sense of connection.

Consider, for instance, a couple nervously attending their first pottery class. Their hands are clumsy, their bowls hilariously misshapen, and the air is filled with bursts of laughter as they fumble through the process. While the clay itself may not yield a masterpiece, what they're truly crafting is a shared story. Each dropped tool or uneven edge becomes a memory, a small triumph or failure that they can laugh about later. These moments of imperfection are far more valuable than the finished product, as they symbolize a willingness to be vulnerable, to try, and to support each other through the process.

Even simple activities, like cooking dinner together, can take on profound meaning when approached with intention. Imagine a couple deciding to recreate a dish from a favorite vacation spot. The act of measuring spices, stirring sauces, and reminiscing about their shared trip turns an ordinary task into a shared adventure. They're not just preparing a meal—they're revisiting memories, collaborating, and creating new ones in the process. Cooking becomes less about perfection and more about the journey: the playful mistakes, the shared effort, and the satisfaction of enjoying something they created together.

While shared experiences lay the groundwork for connection, chemistry is often what ignites the initial spark. Chemistry is that intangible quality that makes interactions feel effortless and exciting. It's the electric thrill of finding someone who finishes your sentences or shares your sense of humor, the way their presence feels like home, even in the earliest stages of knowing them. But as mysterious as it seems, chemistry isn't purely accidental—it's built on subtle psychological cues like shared values, mutual interests, and even nonverbal mirroring.

For example, when someone mirrors your gestures, tone of voice, or energy, it creates a subconscious sense of comfort and alignment. This is why interactive dates, like playing a board game or solving a puzzle together, can often lead to stronger connections. The combination of shared problem-solving and playful banter creates an environment where trust and camaraderie can flourish. These small victories—whether it's winning a game or laughing at a shared mistake—help build the foundation for a lasting connection.

Not all chemistry is immediate or explosive. While some relationships begin with a lightning bolt of attraction, others grow slowly and quietly over time. This is why slower-paced dates that encourage meaningful interaction are just as important as adventurous ones. Picture a couple wandering through an art gallery. At first, their conversation may seem polite, even formal. But as they pause to discuss a particular painting, sharing their personal interpretations or memories it evokes, their chemistry begins to unfold. These quieter moments of intellectual and emotional connection often lay the groundwork for a deeper, more enduring bond.

In these slower moments, couples have the opportunity to truly see and understand each other. The shared exchange of thoughts, feelings, and perspectives creates a sense of intimacy that isn't always present in high-energy settings. Chemistry, in these cases, becomes a steady flame rather than a sudden spark—one that grows stronger with each thoughtful exchange and shared experience.

Memories are the threads that weave the fabric of every relationship. The dates we cherish most are the ones that evoke strong emotions, whether it's joy, awe, or even a touch of nervous excitement. The psychology of memory tells us that experiences tied to heightened emotions are encoded more vividly in our minds. This is why a simple activity like watching a sunset together, with its mix of natural beauty, shared awe, and quiet companionship, can become a cherished memory that lingers for years.

However, memorable dates don't always require elaborate planning or grand gestures. Sometimes, it's the small, thoughtful details that make the biggest impact. A handwritten note slipped into a coat pocket, a song chosen specifically for the moment, or an unexpected gesture like surprising your partner with their favorite dessert can transform an ordinary day into something extraordinary.

These small acts of care and attention show your partner that they are seen, valued, and cherished—turning fleeting moments into lasting memories.

As we draw this chapter to a close, it's important to step back and recognize how the psychology of dating and connection serves as a bridge between everything we've explored so far and the journeys still ahead. Love, after all, isn't a singular event or destination—it's an ever-evolving process, one that thrives on intentionality, understanding, and shared effort. The way we approach dating is a microcosm of how we nurture relationships: by building trust, creating memorable experiences, and showing up authentically.

In Chapter 1, we laid the groundwork for the fundamentals of a great date—learning how to identify what makes our partners feel seen, appreciated, and valued. Those foundational principles taught us that a great date isn't about grand gestures or external perfection but about the thought, care, and emotional resonance we bring to the table. That groundwork carries through to this chapter, where we've uncovered the hidden mechanics that make those moments meaningful. From chemistry to shared experiences to the power of vulnerability, every piece fits together to create a more complete picture of connection.

Similarly, Chapter 2's exploration of creativity and uniqueness in dating aligns perfectly with what we've discussed here. Creativity breathes life into shared experiences, turning everyday moments into adventures and mundane activities into cherished memories. Whether it's trying a new hobby together, revisiting a childhood pastime, or simply daring to step out of your comfort zone, creativity adds an element of novelty and excitement that strengthens the bond between two people. In this chapter, we've examined why those sparks matter so much and how they activate the brain's emotional and reward systems, creating lasting impressions that deepen intimacy.

And, of course, Chapter 3's thematic dates serve as the perfect backdrop for the psychology of connection. Each themed date, whether it's a low-budget picnic or an elaborate holiday-inspired outing, has the potential to engage the elements we've explored here. The laughter over a misstep, the shared awe of a sunset, the quiet joy of holding hands in the glow of festive lights—these moments aren't just nice to have; they're essential. They demonstrate how thoughtful planning and emotional attunement can turn any date into an opportunity to build something lasting.

Now, as we turn the page toward the chapters ahead, it's important to recognize that the insights from this chapter are not isolated—they're the connective tissue that ties past lessons to future possibilities. The next chapter will dive deeper into the long-term dynamics of love: how to revive romance in enduring relationships, navigate the ebbs and flows of connection, and reignite the spark when it begins to dim. But the tools for those endeavors are already here, in the psychology of dating and connection. The same principles that create a great date—intentionality, shared vulnerability, and emotional resonance—are the ones that sustain love over years and decades.

Consider this: the shared laughter of a first date, the nervous excitement of a new adventure, or the quiet comfort of a familiar ritual are not just one-time events. They're building blocks. Each one lays a foundation for something greater—a relationship defined by trust, intimacy, and mutual understanding. Even in the longest relationships, these building blocks remain essential. The dates may evolve, the contexts may change, but the underlying psychology of connection endures.

As we move forward, let's take a moment to reflect on the role of vulnerability in all of this. It's vulnerability that allows us to open up, to let someone see who we truly are, and to build trust that can weather life's inevitable challenges. In new relationships, vulnerability might look like sharing a personal story or admitting a fear. In established ones, it might mean addressing issues honestly or revisiting a shared dream that's been put on hold. The courage to be vulnerable is what transforms fleeting moments into enduring memories, and casual acquaintances into lifelong partners.

At the same time, let's not underestimate the importance of balance—between novelty and familiarity, effort and ease, adventure and quiet. A healthy relationship thrives when there's room for both excitement and stability. The best dates—and the best relationships—combine the thrill of discovery with the comfort of tradition, weaving a rhythm that keeps the connection alive and dynamic.

Ultimately, this chapter is about more than the mechanics of dating; it's about the essence of human connection. It's about understanding that love is both an art and a science, a blend of emotional intuition and psychological insight. It's about seeing every date, every conversation, and every shared experience as an opportunity to build something meaningful. And it's about recognizing that these moments are not isolated—they're part of a greater journey, one that evolves with time but is always rooted in the same principles of care, thoughtfulness, and authenticity.

As you move into the next chapter, consider the ways in which these insights can enrich not just your dating life but your relationship as a whole. Whether you're reigniting the spark in a long-term partnership or building something new, the psychology of connection will always be your guide. It's the foundation for everything that comes next, and it's a reminder that love, at its core, is a shared journey—a story written one moment, one date, one memory at a time.

Reviving Romance in Long-Term Relationships

Every relationship begins with a spark. The early days are often marked by excitement, passion, and the thrill of discovery—a time when everything feels new and effortless. But as the relationship deepens and matures, the initial fireworks settle into a quieter, steadier rhythm. This evolution is both natural and necessary, but it can also bring challenges. The very stability that makes a relationship feel secure can sometimes lead to routine, and the once-vivid spark may begin to flicker. Reviving romance in long-term relationships is not about chasing the intensity of the past but about rediscovering the joy, connection, and intimacy that brought you together in the first place.

In this chapter, we'll explore how to navigate the inevitable shifts that occur in long-term relationships and how to embrace them as opportunities for growth. The goal is not to recreate the past but to build something even stronger—a love that evolves with time, rooted in deep understanding and shared experiences. By recognizing the cycles of connection, learning to communicate effectively, and finding ways to keep curiosity alive, couples can rekindle their romance and deepen their bond.

This chapter builds on the principles of connection and intention from earlier chapters, offering practical tools and insights tailored to the unique challenges of enduring relationships. Whether you're feeling the pull of routine, navigating a period of disconnection, or simply looking to enhance your partnership, the strategies in this chapter will help you reconnect with your partner and reimagine what romance can look like.

We'll begin with the idea that relationships, like nature, go through seasons—and understanding these cycles is the first step in keeping love alive.

Recognizing the Seasons of Love

Long-term relationships, like nature, go through seasons. The early days of infatuation often feel like spring—full of new growth, energy, and the intoxicating bloom of fresh love. Over time, this spring matures into the warmth and steadiness of summer, where passion evolves into a deeper sense of comfort and connection. But just as summer gives way to autumn and winter, relationships too can enter periods of change, challenges, or even dormancy. These seasons are natural and inevitable, yet they are often misunderstood, leading many to mistake a winter season for the end of love.

Understanding the natural rhythm of relationships can shift your perspective and help you navigate periods of stagnation or disconnection with greater compassion and resilience. For example, when the butterflies of early romance fade, it's easy to feel as though something is missing. But this transition from infatuation to stability is a critical step in building a sustainable partnership. It's during this time that love shifts from the excitement of novelty to the richness of familiarity—a kind of love that is less dramatic but far more enduring.

Each season of a relationship brings its own challenges and rewards. Spring, with its excitement and discovery, can also be filled with uncertainty as couples learn about each other. Summer's warmth and stability may feel fulfilling but can sometimes breed complacency if effort isn't maintained. Autumn, a time of reflection, can be an opportunity to celebrate growth while also recognizing areas that need attention. And winter, though often seen as a time of coldness or disconnection, can be a season of rest and renewal, offering the chance to rebuild intimacy and rediscover the spark.

One of the most important lessons in long-term love is learning to embrace these cycles rather than resist them. Periods of distance or challenge do not mean the relationship is failing; they are opportunities for growth. Just as winter prepares the ground for spring, moments of disconnection can pave the way for a deeper, more meaningful connection—if approached with patience and intention.

Couples who recognize these seasons and adapt to them are better equipped to sustain their relationship through life's inevitable ups and downs. For example, a couple in the "autumn" of their relationship might take time to reflect on the journey they've shared, expressing gratitude for their partner while acknowledging the changes they've both experienced. In contrast, a couple in a "winter" phase might focus on small acts of kindness and communication to thaw emotional distance and prepare for a new spring of connection.

It's also essential to understand that not all seasons occur simultaneously for both partners. One partner may feel they are in the steady comfort of summer, while the other feels stuck in the reflective autumn. These differences can create tension, but they can also open the door to important conversations about individual needs and shared goals. By acknowledging where each partner stands, couples can work together to bridge the gap and move forward with greater unity.

Recognizing the seasons of love doesn't mean accepting disconnection or stagnation as permanent—it means understanding that these phases are temporary and provide the groundwork for transformation. Each season offers its own beauty and lessons. Spring reminds us of the joy of discovery, summer celebrates the warmth of stability, autumn encourages reflection and gratitude, and winter challenges us to find strength and renewal. Together, these cycles create the rhythm of a relationship that is not just enduring but thriving.

The Power of Small Gestures

In the context of long-term relationships, romance is not always about grand displays of affection. Instead, it thrives in the small, meaningful gestures that remind your partner they are loved and appreciated. These acts might seem insignificant on the surface, but they carry profound emotional weight, serving as daily reminders of connection and care. A small gesture, done thoughtfully, can bridge emotional distances, reignite intimacy, and keep the foundation of love strong.

Consider this: a busy couple navigating the chaos of daily life might not always have time for elaborate dates or extended conversations. Yet, a simple gesture—a note tucked into a lunch bag, a favorite coffee waiting on the counter, or an unexpected compliment—can remind one partner of the other's love in a tangible way. These small acts are anchors, grounding a relationship in moments of kindness and consideration, even amidst the hustle and noise of everyday life.

Small gestures are also powerful because they don't require perfect timing or special occasions. They can happen spontaneously, making them feel more genuine and heartfelt. Imagine a partner who, knowing you've had a stressful day, lights a candle and draws a bath without being asked. Or one who texts during a busy workday just to say, "Thinking of you." These actions don't just brighten the moment; they create a sense of being seen and valued, reinforcing the emotional connection that long-term relationships rely on.

Another reason small gestures matter is that they often align with a partner's love language. For some, an unexpected hug or touch on the shoulder speaks volumes. For others, a tiny act of service—like tidying a cluttered space or running an errand—feels like an expression of care. By tuning into your partner's unique preferences and habits, you can use these gestures to communicate love in a way that feels deeply personal and meaningful.

It's also important to recognize that small gestures are not one-size-fits-all; they are most effective when they reflect the individual dynamics of your relationship. A couple that bonded over shared humor might find joy in leaving silly notes for each other. Another couple, whose connection is rooted in deep conversation, might prioritize sending thoughtful texts or sharing articles that resonate. The key is to personalize these actions so they feel authentic and connected to your shared story.

Beyond their immediate impact, small gestures have a cumulative effect. Over time, they create a reservoir of positive memories and emotions that couples can draw on during more challenging times. When conflicts arise or life becomes overwhelming, these seemingly minor acts can serve as reminders of the care and effort that both partners bring to the relationship. They build a sense of goodwill, making it easier to weather storms and bounce back from moments of disconnection.

Small gestures also encourage reciprocity, creating a cycle of giving and receiving that strengthens the relationship. When one partner consistently makes an effort to show care, the other is often inspired to do the same. This mutual reinforcement fosters a culture of appreciation and kindness, ensuring that both partners feel valued and supported. Over time, this practice of small, intentional acts becomes woven into the fabric of the relationship, turning everyday moments into opportunities for connection.

In the end, small gestures are far from trivial. They are the quiet, consistent acts of love that keep the flame alive in long-term relationships. By prioritizing these moments of care, couples can maintain a sense of romance and intimacy, even in the face of life's inevitable demands. The power of these gestures lies in their ability to transform the ordinary into the extraordinary, reminding both partners that love is found not just in grand events but in the daily rhythms of shared life.

Rekindling Curiosity

One of the most common challenges in long-term relationships is the slow erosion of curiosity. Over time, familiarity can create the illusion that you already know everything there is to know about your partner. The stories they've shared, the habits you've observed, and the routines you've built together may seem to leave little room for discovery. Yet, the truth is that people are constantly evolving, shaped by new experiences, ideas, and dreams. Rekindling curiosity is about seeing your partner not as someone static but as a dynamic individual, full of layers waiting to be uncovered.

Curiosity is the foundation of connection. It is what drives us to ask questions, explore new perspectives, and engage in meaningful conversations. When couples stop being curious about each other, the relationship risks becoming stagnant. To prevent this, it's essential to cultivate a sense of wonder—not just about your partner but also about the life you're building together. Curiosity turns mundane interactions into opportunities for deeper understanding, helping couples rediscover the richness of their bond.

One way to rekindle curiosity is to ask new questions. Even if you've been together for years, there are always unexplored topics or forgotten dreams that can spark fresh conversations. Try asking your partner, "What's a goal you've been thinking about recently?" or "If you could live anywhere in the world, where would it be?" These kinds of questions invite your partner to share their current aspirations and thoughts, creating space for connection and discovery.

Another approach is to reflect on how your partner has changed over time. The person you fell in love with may still have the same core values, but their interests, preferences, and outlook on life have likely evolved. By paying attention to these shifts, you can better understand who they are today—and who they are becoming. This might involve noticing small changes, like their new favorite coffee order, or deeper transformations, like a shift in career goals or personal priorities.

Rekindling curiosity also extends to shared experiences. Trying something new together—a hobby, a class, or even a type of cuisine—can reignite the sense of adventure that often characterizes the early stages of a relationship. For example, taking a dance class or exploring a nearby city you've never visited allows you to see your partner in a new light. How do they respond to challenges? What makes them light up with excitement? These experiences create opportunities to learn about each other in ways that are both fun and meaningful.

Another powerful way to fuel curiosity is through shared storytelling. Reflecting on past experiences together—especially ones that haven't been discussed in a while—can uncover new insights. You might revisit memories from when you first met, sharing how those moments felt from each of your perspectives. Or, you could dig deeper into stories from your partner's childhood, asking questions about their favorite traditions or pivotal moments. These conversations can reveal layers of understanding that deepen your connection.

Curiosity isn't just about asking questions; it's about listening with genuine interest. When your partner shares something, approach it with an open heart and mind. Resist the urge to jump to conclusions or assume you already know their answer. Instead, focus on their words, their emotions, and the meaning behind what they're saying. Active listening is a form of curiosity in action, showing your partner that you value their thoughts and experiences.

Finally, rekindling curiosity is about cultivating a mindset of discovery in your daily interactions. Rather than seeing your partner as someone you "know," view them as someone you're always getting to know. This mindset fosters a sense of appreciation and excitement, reminding you that your partner is a dynamic, multifaceted person with endless layers to explore. Even small changes in how you approach conversations—like asking open-ended questions or expressing enthusiasm for their ideas—can make a big difference.

In long-term relationships, curiosity is the spark that keeps love vibrant and evolving. By staying open to learning about your partner and creating opportunities for shared exploration, you can deepen your connection and strengthen your bond. In the end, curiosity isn't just about rediscovering your partner—it's about rediscovering the joy of growing together.

Navigating Conflict and Building Resilience

No relationship is immune to conflict. Disagreements, misunderstandings, and emotional rough patches are inevitable when two individuals share their lives. However, it's not the presence of conflict that determines the strength of a relationship—it's how couples navigate it. Healthy conflict resolution is an opportunity to build resilience, strengthen trust, and deepen intimacy. When approached with care and intentionality, even the most challenging conversations can lead to growth and a stronger connection.

The first step in navigating conflict is reframing it. Instead of viewing disagreements as threats to the relationship, see them as opportunities for understanding and collaboration. Conflict often arises when unspoken needs or feelings come to the surface, signaling that something in the relationship requires attention. By approaching these moments with curiosity rather than defensiveness, couples can transform arguments into constructive discussions. This shift in perspective helps reduce feelings of blame and creates a foundation for mutual problem-solving.

Effective communication is the cornerstone of healthy conflict resolution. This means expressing yourself honestly while remaining mindful of your partner's emotions. Instead of using accusatory language, focus on "I" statements that convey your feelings without assigning blame. For example, instead of saying, "You never listen to me," you might say, "I feel unheard when we don't discuss things fully." This approach invites your partner into the conversation rather than putting them on the defensive.

Equally important is the ability to listen actively and empathetically. When your partner shares their perspective, resist the urge to interrupt or formulate a response before they've finished speaking. Instead, focus on understanding their feelings and motivations. Reflecting back what you've heard—such as, "It sounds like you're feeling frustrated because..." —can help clarify misunderstandings and show your partner that their feelings are valid and important.

Another essential aspect of navigating conflict is recognizing and addressing underlying patterns. Many couples find themselves having the same argument repeatedly, often because the core issue remains unresolved. These recurring conflicts can stem from deeper insecurities, unmet needs, or differences in communication styles. Identifying these patterns allows couples to address the root cause rather than just the surface disagreement. This might involve discussing individual triggers, exploring past experiences that influence current behaviors, or seeking professional support if needed.

Resilience in relationships also comes from learning to repair after conflict. Every argument, no matter how well-managed, can leave emotional residue that needs to be addressed. Repairing doesn't mean pretending the disagreement never happened; it means acknowledging the hurt, taking responsibility for your actions, and finding ways to rebuild trust. A sincere apology, a gesture of reconciliation, or simply checking in with your partner after the dust has settled can go a long way in restoring harmony.

Forgiveness plays a key role in this process. Holding onto resentment or grudges can create emotional distance, eroding intimacy over time. Forgiveness doesn't mean condoning hurtful behavior or ignoring your own feelings—it means choosing to let go of the emotional weight that prevents you from moving forward. In forgiving your partner, you make space for healing and reaffirm your commitment to the relationship.

Conflict also provides an opportunity for couples to grow closer by learning from each other. Disagreements often reveal differences in values, priorities, or communication styles that might not have been evident otherwise. By exploring these differences with openness and respect, couples can gain a deeper understanding of each other's perspectives. This process not only resolves the immediate issue but also strengthens the relationship's ability to handle future challenges.

Finally, navigating conflict requires a commitment to resilience. Resilience doesn't mean avoiding difficulties—it means facing them together, with the belief that the relationship is worth the effort. It involves creating a culture of mutual support, where both partners feel safe expressing their emotions and working through disagreements. Over time, this shared commitment builds a stronger, more trusting bond.

In long-term relationships, conflict is not a sign of failure but a natural part of growth. By embracing these moments as opportunities to learn and connect, couples can build a foundation of resilience that sustains their love through life's inevitable ups and downs. In this way, navigating conflict becomes not just a challenge but a pathway to deeper intimacy and understanding.

Physical Intimacy and Emotional Connection

Physical intimacy and emotional connection are deeply intertwined, forming two pillars that support the foundation of any long-term relationship. While physical touch often serves as a primary expression of love and affection, it's the emotional bond between partners that makes intimacy truly meaningful. Over time, as relationships mature, these elements may evolve—but maintaining a balance between them is essential to keep the connection alive and thriving.

Physical intimacy is more than just sexual activity. It encompasses all forms of touch that communicate love, care, and presence—holding hands during a walk, a kiss on the forehead, a warm embrace after a long day. These gestures foster a sense of security and belonging, reminding your partner that you're emotionally and physically present. Research has shown that even small acts of touch can release oxytocin, the "bonding hormone," which strengthens feelings of trust and attachment.

However, physical intimacy in long-term relationships often shifts as life circumstances change. Work stress, parenting responsibilities, health issues, and aging can all impact the frequency or nature of physical connection. These changes are natural, but they require conscious effort to navigate. When couples feel disconnected physically, it's often a reflection of an underlying emotional gap. Addressing this emotional distance is the first step toward rebuilding physical closeness.

Reconnecting emotionally involves open and honest communication about needs, desires, and fears. Partners may hesitate to discuss intimacy, worrying about embarrassment or rejection, but these conversations are vital. Talking about what makes you feel connected, what you miss, and what you'd like to explore together can reignite the physical side of the relationship. For example, a partner might express a longing for more non-sexual touch, like cuddling on the couch or spontaneous hugs, while the other might feel more fulfilled by planning intentional date nights that lead to intimacy.

It's also important to recognize that emotional connection often precedes physical intimacy, especially in long-term relationships. Emotional connection is built through shared experiences, meaningful conversations, and acts of vulnerability. For instance, a partner who feels supported during a difficult time—whether through attentive listening, encouragement, or small gestures of care—is more likely to feel drawn to their partner physically. Emotional intimacy creates a safe space where physical closeness can flourish naturally.

Another key element in maintaining physical intimacy is prioritizing quality over quantity. In the early stages of a relationship, passion is often fueled by novelty and the excitement of discovery. Over time, as familiarity grows, the focus shifts from intensity to depth. Intimate moments don't have to be frequent or elaborate to be meaningful—they just need to be intentional. Setting aside time to connect, even in small ways, can make a significant difference. For example, a simple ritual like sharing a kiss before bed or holding hands during a movie can rekindle feelings of closeness.

Reinvigorating physical intimacy can also involve trying new things together. This doesn't necessarily mean grand gestures but rather small changes that bring excitement and playfulness back into the relationship. Perhaps you experiment with a dance class that gets you moving together or plan a weekend getaway that allows for uninterrupted time to reconnect. The act of exploring something new can reignite the sense of adventure and passion that often fades over time.

It's equally important to acknowledge that physical intimacy is not always easy for everyone. Past experiences, body image concerns, or unresolved conflicts can create barriers to closeness. Addressing these issues—whether through self-reflection, couples' counseling, or open communication—can help break down those barriers and pave the way for greater connection. A supportive partner who listens without judgment and approaches intimacy with patience and empathy can create an environment where both partners feel safe to express themselves fully.

Finally, physical intimacy is a practice, not a destination. It requires ongoing effort and intention to adapt to the changes and challenges that come with time. By fostering emotional connection, communicating openly, and making space for physical closeness, couples can create a relationship where intimacy is not just sustained but continually renewed. This interplay between emotional and physical connection transforms intimacy from a fleeting spark into a steady, enduring flame.

In long-term relationships, physical intimacy is not about recreating the intensity of the past but about embracing the evolution of your connection. By staying attuned to each other's needs and finding ways to bridge emotional and physical closeness, you can cultivate a partnership that grows richer and more fulfilling with each passing year.

Reinventing Traditions

Traditions are the threads that weave together the shared history of a relationship, providing a sense of stability and continuity. Over time, these rituals—whether grand celebrations or quiet, personal habits—become touchstones of connection. However, as relationships grow and life changes, these traditions may begin to lose their vibrancy. Reinventing traditions is about finding ways to honor the past while embracing the present, ensuring that your rituals evolve alongside your relationship.

At the heart of every tradition is meaning. It's not the act itself—whether it's a weekly date night, an annual holiday tradition, or a simple morning coffee routine—that creates connection, but the emotional resonance it carries. These rituals serve as reminders of your commitment and shared values. For example, a couple might have a tradition of cooking together every Friday evening. Over time, this activity becomes more than just preparing a meal; it's a dedicated moment to reconnect after a busy week, creating space for laughter, conversation, and teamwork.

However, as life circumstances shift—careers evolve, children are born, or external stressors increase—old traditions may no longer fit. What once felt special might now feel routine or even burdensome. Recognizing when a tradition needs to be refreshed is crucial to keeping it meaningful. For instance, a couple who used to celebrate every anniversary with a fancy dinner may find that this no longer feels practical or enjoyable. Instead, they might create a new tradition, such as spending the day exploring a new city or writing letters to each other reflecting on the past year.

Reinventing traditions doesn't mean discarding old ones entirely. It's about adapting them to your current stage of life and relationship. This process often begins with revisiting the purpose behind a ritual. Ask yourselves: What does this tradition mean to us? Why did we start it? How can we make it feel relevant now? By focusing on the emotional core of the tradition, you can find ways to preserve its essence while making it more aligned with your present needs and circumstances.

Creating new traditions can also be a powerful way to inject excitement and novelty into your relationship. These rituals don't have to be elaborate; they simply need to reflect your shared interests and values. For example, a couple might decide to start a tradition of trying a new recipe every Sunday or taking a spontaneous road trip each summer. The key is to choose activities that feel meaningful and enjoyable for both partners, ensuring that the tradition strengthens your bond rather than feeling like an obligation.

Another way to reinvent traditions is to involve collaboration and creativity. Instead of one partner always planning a particular event, make it a joint effort. For instance, if you have a tradition of watching holiday movies every December, you might alternate who gets to pick the movie or add a new twist, like creating a themed snack to go with it. By involving both partners in the process, you ensure that the tradition continues to feel fresh and engaging.

It's also important to recognize that traditions can be powerful tools for navigating change and challenges. During difficult times, familiar rituals provide a sense of comfort and stability. For example, a couple going through a stressful period might find solace in their tradition of a nightly walk together. Reinventing traditions during these moments can also help couples adapt to new realities. A family facing financial difficulties, for instance, might replace an expensive holiday trip with a cozy stay-at-home celebration, focusing on connection rather than cost.

In long-term relationships, traditions are opportunities to celebrate both your shared history and your evolving journey. They remind you of where you've been while creating space to imagine where you're going. By approaching traditions with flexibility and creativity, couples can ensure that their rituals continue to feel meaningful and enriching, no matter what life brings.

Ultimately, reinventing traditions is about keeping the spark of connection alive through intentionality and effort. It's a chance to reaffirm your commitment to each other while embracing the changes that come with time. Whether you're revisiting old rituals or creating new ones, the goal is the same: to nurture a relationship that is dynamic, enduring, and full of shared meaning.

Romance in long-term relationships is not a fleeting spark to be chased but a steady flame to be tended. It's a dynamic force that evolves as you and your partner grow, shaped by the rhythms of life, the challenges you face together, and the love you cultivate through intentional actions. This chapter has shown that rekindling romance is not about grand gestures or returning to the honeymoon phase but about creating meaningful moments, embracing change, and deepening your connection in ways that reflect the strength and history of your bond.

We began by recognizing the seasons of love, understanding that relationships naturally go through cycles of warmth, reflection, and renewal. Just as nature's seasons bring different opportunities for growth, so too do the phases of a relationship. Viewing these shifts not as signs of failure but as opportunities for growth allows couples to approach challenges with compassion and resilience, preparing the ground for the next chapter of their love story.

From there, we explored the power of small gestures—those quiet, everyday acts of kindness and thoughtfulness that remind your partner they are seen, valued, and cherished. These gestures are the lifeblood of a lasting relationship, turning ordinary moments into extraordinary opportunities for connection. They build a reservoir of goodwill, fostering a culture of appreciation and care that strengthens the relationship over time.

Rekindling curiosity reminded us of the importance of never stopping the process of discovery. Long-term relationships thrive when partners continue to see each other as dynamic individuals, full of new thoughts, dreams, and layers to uncover. Asking questions, exploring shared experiences, and reflecting on how you've both grown create a sense of excitement and wonder that keeps love vibrant and evolving.

We also delved into the inevitable conflicts that arise in any partnership, recognizing them not as threats but as chances to strengthen your bond. Navigating conflict with empathy, honesty, and a willingness to repair builds resilience, transforming moments of tension into opportunities for deeper understanding. The ability to move through challenges together reaffirms your commitment and reminds you both that your relationship is worth the effort.

Physical intimacy and emotional connection are deeply intertwined, forming the foundation for lasting romance. This chapter emphasized that intimacy evolves over time, requiring effort, communication, and a shared willingness to adapt. By prioritizing emotional closeness and approaching physical intimacy with curiosity and care, couples can cultivate a connection that feels both enduring and renewing.

Finally, reinventing traditions reminded us of the power of rituals to anchor a relationship through life's changes. Traditions are not static; they are living expressions of your shared values and history. By revisiting, refreshing, or creating new rituals, couples can celebrate their journey while embracing the present and looking ahead to the future.

Taken together, these elements form a comprehensive roadmap for reviving and sustaining romance in long-term relationships. Each strategy, from small gestures to reinvented traditions, reinforces the idea that love is not a passive state but an active choice—a commitment to showing up for each other, day after day, in ways that nurture connection and intimacy.

As we look ahead to the next chapter, where we will explore resilience and personal growth through the lens of relationships, remember that the foundation for any transformative change begins here, with intention and effort. Reviving romance is not just about rekindling what was once there; it's about building something new—something even stronger and more meaningful than before. It's a testament to the enduring power of love to grow, evolve, and thrive, no matter where the journey takes you.

Navigating Challenges and Building Resilience

Every relationship, no matter how strong or loving, will encounter challenges. These moments of tension and disagreement are not only inevitable—they're essential to growth. Just as friction polishes a stone, conflict can strengthen a relationship when approached with the right mindset. The real measure of a successful partnership isn't the absence of conflict but the ability to navigate it with empathy, understanding, and a shared commitment to resolution.

Conflict often gets a bad reputation. It can feel uncomfortable, even threatening, to confront differences or acknowledge tension in a relationship. However, avoiding conflict entirely can lead to unresolved issues that fester beneath the surface, creating distance between partners over time. Instead, embracing challenges as opportunities to learn and grow together fosters resilience, trust, and deeper intimacy.

This chapter explores how couples can move through difficult moments with intention and care, turning challenges into stepping stones rather than stumbling blocks. From understanding the root causes of conflict to fostering empathy and teamwork, the strategies in this chapter provide a framework for navigating tough times together. The journey begins with a deeper look at the nature of conflict itself—why it arises, what it reveals, and how it can become a powerful tool for connection.

Understanding the Nature of Conflict

Conflict is an inevitable part of any relationship. It arises from differences in perspectives, unmet expectations, or emotional triggers, and it can feel uncomfortable, even painful, in the moment. But conflict, when approached with care and understanding, is not something to fear—it's an opportunity to learn about your partner, yourself, and the dynamics of your relationship. Understanding the nature of conflict is the first step in transforming it from a source of tension into a pathway for growth and connection.

The first thing to recognize is that not all conflict is the same. Healthy conflict is a natural and necessary part of a relationship. It often involves productive discussions about differences in values, goals, or emotions, where both partners feel safe to express themselves without fear of judgment. Healthy conflict challenges couples to explore new perspectives, find compromises, and strengthen their bond. On the other hand, unhealthy conflict is characterized by destructive communication patterns, such as blame, criticism, or defensiveness, which can erode trust and emotional safety over time. Recognizing the difference is key to navigating disagreements constructively.

Another important aspect of conflict is understanding its root causes. Surface-level arguments—like who forgot to take out the trash or why someone didn't respond to a text—often mask deeper issues. These could include feelings of neglect, unmet emotional needs, or underlying stress from external factors like work or family obligations. For example, a disagreement about household chores might actually reflect a partner's need to feel appreciated for their contributions or their frustration over feeling overwhelmed. By looking beyond the immediate issue and exploring the emotions driving the conflict, couples can address the real problem rather than getting stuck in repetitive arguments.

Conflict is also influenced by individual emotional triggers. These triggers are often shaped by past experiences, personal insecurities, or deeply held values. For instance, one partner might feel particularly sensitive to interruptions during conversations because they grew up in an environment where their voice wasn't valued. Another might struggle with criticism because it reminds them of a history of harsh judgment. Understanding your own triggers—and learning about your partner's—can help you navigate conflict with greater empathy and self-awareness. It allows you to respond thoughtfully rather than react impulsively, reducing the likelihood of escalating tension.

External factors also play a significant role in shaping conflict. Stress from work, financial difficulties, or health challenges can spill into the relationship, amplifying misunderstandings and emotional responses. For example, a partner who is preoccupied with job insecurity may seem distant or irritable, leading the other partner to feel neglected or unimportant. Recognizing when external pressures are influencing internal dynamics helps couples avoid misattributing blame and instead work together to address the root cause.

Understanding the nature of conflict also means acknowledging its cyclical patterns. Many couples find themselves having the same argument repeatedly, often because they haven't addressed the underlying issue. These recurring conflicts can create feelings of frustration and hopelessness, making it seem like the relationship is stuck in a negative loop. Breaking these cycles requires a willingness to reflect on past disagreements, identify common themes, and explore what each partner truly needs to feel heard and understood. For example, if arguments about time management keep resurfacing, it may signal a deeper need for shared priorities or better communication about schedules.

A critical aspect of navigating conflict is recognizing that it doesn't always need to be resolved immediately. Sometimes, taking a step back to cool down and reflect can prevent impulsive reactions and create space for more thoughtful dialogue. Pausing doesn't mean ignoring the issue; it means prioritizing the health of the relationship over the urgency of the argument. Couples who practice this approach often find that they're able to return to the conversation with greater clarity and empathy.

Ultimately, understanding the nature of conflict is about seeing it as a natural and necessary part of a relationship. Conflict is not a sign of failure but a signal that something needs attention—whether it's a difference in values, an emotional need, or an external stressor. By approaching conflict with curiosity and compassion, couples can transform it into an opportunity for growth, deepening their connection and building a stronger foundation for the future.

Building Emotional Resilience

Resilience is the ability to adapt, recover, and grow stronger in the face of adversity. In relationships, emotional resilience is the foundation that allows couples to weather challenges together, transforming obstacles into opportunities for deeper connection. It's not about avoiding difficulties but about cultivating the tools and mindset to face them with courage, compassion, and a sense of partnership. Building emotional resilience requires both individual growth and mutual effort, creating a bond that can withstand life's inevitable ups and downs.

At the heart of emotional resilience lies self-awareness. Understanding your own emotional patterns, triggers, and coping mechanisms is crucial for navigating conflict and stress in a relationship. For example, recognizing that you tend to shut down during arguments can help you communicate this tendency to your partner, allowing them to respond with patience rather than frustration. Similarly, identifying when your emotions are heightened by external stressors—like work deadlines or family pressures—enables you to address those issues proactively, rather than letting them spill into your relationship.

Resilience also involves emotional regulation, the ability to manage intense feelings without being overwhelmed by them. In moments of conflict or stress, it's easy to react impulsively, saying or doing things that might hurt your partner or escalate the situation. Practicing techniques like deep breathing, pausing before responding, or journaling your thoughts can help you stay grounded and approach challenges with clarity. By modeling this behavior, you encourage your partner to do the same, creating an environment of mutual respect and emotional safety.

A growth mindset is another key component of resilience. Instead of viewing challenges as insurmountable problems, couples with a growth mindset see them as opportunities to learn and strengthen their bond. This perspective shifts the focus from blame or defeat to collaboration and problem-solving. For example, if a couple is struggling with communication, adopting a growth mindset might involve seeking out resources, such as relationship books or counseling, to develop new skills together. This proactive approach not only addresses the issue but also demonstrates a shared commitment to the relationship.

Emotional resilience also thrives on mutual support. While it's important to cultivate your own coping strategies, resilience in a relationship depends on both partners being willing to lean on each other during difficult times. This might mean offering a listening ear when your partner needs to vent, stepping in to ease their burdens when they're overwhelmed, or simply reminding them that you're in this together. These acts of support build trust and reinforce the idea that the relationship is a safe haven, even in the midst of challenges.

Another essential element of resilience is adaptability. Life is full of unexpected changes—new jobs, health challenges, relocations, or shifts in family dynamics—that can disrupt the balance of a relationship. Couples who are able to adapt to these changes with flexibility and an open mind are more likely to thrive in the long run. Adaptability doesn't mean ignoring the difficulties of change; it means working together to find new rhythms and solutions that align with your shared goals and values.

Resilience is also strengthened by cultivating moments of joy and gratitude, even in the midst of challenges. When life feels heavy, taking time to celebrate small victories, share a laugh, or express appreciation for your partner can provide a sense of balance and perspective. For example, a couple navigating financial difficulties might find comfort in a simple tradition, like cooking dinner together at home, transforming what could feel like a restriction into an opportunity for connection. These moments of positivity act as emotional anchors, reminding you both of the love and strength that underpin your relationship.

Finally, resilience is not about perfection; it's about persistence. No couple navigates every challenge flawlessly, and mistakes are inevitable. What matters is the willingness to reflect, learn, and try again. When you approach challenges with this mindset, each obstacle becomes a stepping stone toward greater understanding and intimacy. By building emotional resilience, you and your partner create a relationship that not only survives difficulties but thrives because of them.

In the end, emotional resilience is a practice—a skill that grows stronger with time, intention, and effort. By focusing on self-awareness, emotional regulation, mutual support, and adaptability, couples can face life's challenges with confidence and unity. This resilience becomes the foundation for a relationship that is not only enduring but deeply fulfilling, built on a shared belief in the power of love to overcome even the toughest trials.

The Power of Empathy and Active Listening

Empathy and active listening are the cornerstones of effective communication in any relationship. They provide the foundation for understanding, validation, and emotional connection, especially during moments of conflict or stress. In long-term relationships, where differences can sometimes feel magnified by years of shared experiences, the ability to truly hear and empathize with your partner becomes an essential skill. This section explores how cultivating empathy and practicing active listening can transform even the most difficult conversations into opportunities for growth and connection.

Empathy begins with the ability to see a situation from your partner's perspective. This doesn't mean you have to agree with them, but it does require setting aside your own assumptions and judgments long enough to genuinely consider how they feel. For example, if your partner seems distant after a disagreement, rather than assuming they're ignoring you, empathy might lead you to ask, "Are you feeling hurt or overwhelmed right now?" By approaching the situation with curiosity instead of defensiveness, you create a space for understanding and connection.

Active listening is the practice of fully focusing on your partner's words, emotions, and nonverbal cues. It's more than just hearing what they say—it's about engaging with their message in a way that makes them feel seen and valued. This requires putting aside distractions, such as your phone or your own inner dialogue, and giving your partner your undivided attention. A simple but powerful phrase like, "I hear you," can reassure them that their feelings matter and that you are present in the conversation.

One of the most important aspects of active listening is validation. Validation doesn't mean agreeing with everything your partner says; it means acknowledging their feelings and experiences as legitimate. For instance, if your partner expresses frustration about a stressful day, saying, "That sounds really difficult. I can see why you'd feel that way," shows that you're attuned to their emotions. Validation helps diffuse tension and reassures your partner that their emotions are respected, even if your perspective differs.

Empathy and active listening are particularly valuable in moments of conflict. When emotions run high, it's easy to fall into the trap of defending your own position rather than truly hearing your partner's concerns. However, this often leads to misunderstandings and escalation. Instead, try reflecting their feelings back to them before responding. For example, if your partner says, "I feel like you don't prioritize our time together," you might respond, "It sounds like you're feeling unimportant or neglected. Is that right?" This reflection not only clarifies their feelings but also shows that you're making an effort to understand their perspective.

Another critical component of empathy is recognizing and addressing emotional needs. Sometimes, what your partner says on the surface may not fully convey what they're feeling underneath. For example, if they express frustration about household chores, their deeper need might be for recognition and appreciation rather than just logistical support. Asking follow-up questions like, "Is there something more you'd like me to understand?" can help uncover these underlying emotions, fostering deeper connection.

Nonverbal communication is also a powerful tool in active listening. Eye contact, a nod of understanding, or a comforting touch can convey empathy even when words fall short. These small gestures reinforce that you're fully present and engaged in the conversation. Conversely, avoiding eye contact, interrupting, or showing impatience can signal disinterest, even if that's not your intention. Being mindful of your nonverbal cues helps ensure that your actions align with your words.

Empathy and active listening also require emotional regulation. When faced with criticism or intense emotions from your partner, it's natural to feel defensive. However, reacting impulsively can derail the conversation and deepen the conflict. Taking a moment to breathe, reflect, and remind yourself that your partner's feelings are valid—even if their delivery isn't perfect—can help you respond with compassion rather than defensiveness.

Practicing empathy and active listening takes time and effort, but the rewards are profound. These skills not only help resolve conflicts more effectively but also strengthen the emotional bond between partners. They create a sense of safety and trust, where both individuals feel valued and understood. Over time, this foundation of empathy fosters deeper intimacy, making it easier to navigate future challenges together.

Ultimately, empathy and active listening are acts of love. They demonstrate a willingness to prioritize your partner's feelings and experiences, even when it's difficult. By consistently showing up for each other in this way, couples can build a relationship that is not only resilient but also deeply fulfilling—a partnership rooted in understanding, compassion, and mutual respect.

Teamwork and Shared Problem-Solving

A strong relationship thrives when both partners see themselves as a team, working together to overcome challenges and achieve shared goals. Teamwork and shared problem-solving are not just practical tools—they are foundational to building trust, fostering unity, and deepening the bond between two people. When life presents obstacles, approaching them as a team rather than as individuals with competing interests can transform even the most daunting problems into opportunities for growth and connection.

At the core of teamwork is the mindset that it's "us versus the problem," not "me versus you." This shift in perspective is critical in long-term relationships. When partners view challenges as shared experiences rather than individual burdens, they're more likely to approach them collaboratively. For example, if a couple is dealing with financial stress, framing the issue as "How can we tackle this together?" rather than "Why aren't you earning more?" fosters cooperation and reduces the risk of blame and resentment.

Effective teamwork begins with clear communication. Partners need to articulate their thoughts, feelings, and expectations in a way that invites dialogue rather than defensiveness. This involves not only expressing your perspective but also actively listening to your partner's. For instance, if one partner feels overwhelmed by household responsibilities, they might say, "I've been feeling really stressed about managing the chores lately. Can we find a way to divide them more evenly?" This approach opens the door to a collaborative solution rather than fueling frustration.

Shared problem-solving is also about recognizing each other's strengths and utilizing them effectively. Every individual brings unique skills, experiences, and perspectives to the table. For example, one partner might excel at budgeting while the other has a knack for planning and organizing. By dividing responsibilities in a way that plays to each partner's strengths, couples can address challenges more efficiently and with less stress. This division of labor not only lightens the load but also reinforces the sense of partnership and mutual support.

Conflict resolution is another critical component of teamwork. In many cases, disagreements arise because partners approach problems with different priorities or solutions. Rather than insisting on being "right," couples who prioritize teamwork focus on finding compromises that work for both parties. This might involve brainstorming multiple solutions and discussing the pros and cons of each, ensuring that both voices are heard and valued. For instance, a couple debating how to spend a weekend might agree to alternate between their preferences, balancing relaxation with adventure.

Teamwork also requires flexibility and adaptability. Life rarely goes according to plan, and unexpected challenges can throw even the most well-organized couples off course. In these moments, the ability to pivot and adjust together is crucial. For example, if a planned vacation is canceled due to unforeseen circumstances, a resilient couple might work together to create an alternative experience, such as a staycation filled with creative activities. This adaptability not only resolves the immediate issue but also reinforces the couple's ability to face adversity as a unit.

A key aspect of shared problem-solving is maintaining a sense of fairness and equity. When one partner consistently shoulders more of the emotional or practical burden, resentment can build, undermining the relationship. Regularly checking in with each other about how responsibilities are divided ensures that both partners feel supported and valued. This might involve having honest conversations about workload or adjusting expectations during particularly stressful periods. For instance, if one partner is facing a demanding work schedule, the other might temporarily take on more household tasks to balance the load.

Another essential element of teamwork is celebrating successes together, no matter how small. Acknowledging your collective efforts and victories reinforces the idea that you're in this together. For example, if a couple successfully navigates a challenging financial period, taking a moment to reflect on their teamwork and celebrate their progress—whether with a heartfelt conversation or a shared treat—can strengthen their bond and provide motivation for future challenges.

Teamwork also requires patience and understanding. No two people will always agree, and disagreements are a natural part of problem-solving. The goal is not to avoid conflict altogether but to approach it with respect and a shared commitment to resolution. This might involve stepping back when emotions run high, revisiting the conversation with a clearer mind, or seeking outside support, such as counseling, when necessary.

Ultimately, teamwork and shared problem-solving are about fostering a partnership where both individuals feel empowered, valued, and supported. By approaching challenges with unity, couples can build a relationship that not only survives adversity but thrives because of it. The strength of a relationship lies not in the absence of problems but in the way partners come together to face them, hand in hand, as a team.

Rebuilding Trust After Challenges

Trust is the cornerstone of any strong relationship, but it's also one of the most fragile elements. When trust is broken—whether through small breaches like forgotten promises or significant betrayals like dishonesty or infidelity—it can feel like the foundation of the relationship has been shaken. Rebuilding trust after challenges is a delicate but achievable process that requires time, effort, and mutual commitment. It's not about erasing the past but about creating a new foundation of honesty, respect, and accountability.

The first step in rebuilding trust is acknowledging the breach. This requires both partners to confront the issue openly and honestly. For the partner who caused the breach, this means taking full responsibility for their actions without deflecting blame or minimizing the impact. A sincere apology is essential, but it must go beyond words. Actions that demonstrate accountability—such as following through on commitments, showing consistency, and being transparent—are what truly begin to rebuild trust.

For the partner who feels betrayed, expressing emotions openly is just as important. Suppressing anger, sadness, or disappointment can create emotional distance and hinder the healing process. Instead, it's essential to communicate these feelings in a way that invites dialogue rather than escalating conflict. Saying something like, "I feel hurt because I trusted you to be honest with me, and now I'm struggling to feel safe in our relationship," creates a space for vulnerability and understanding. This expression of emotion can help both partners begin to navigate the path toward healing.

Rebuilding trust also involves establishing clear boundaries and expectations moving forward. These boundaries provide a sense of security and structure, helping both partners rebuild confidence in the relationship. For example, if the breach of trust involved dishonesty about finances, a couple might agree to adopt a more transparent approach to budgeting and spending, such as sharing access to accounts or setting regular check-ins about financial decisions. These steps create accountability and demonstrate a commitment to regaining trust.

Patience is another critical element of rebuilding trust. Healing takes time, and both partners must be willing to move through the process at a pace that feels right for them. For the partner who feels betrayed, this means allowing themselves the time to rebuild their sense of safety and confidence. For the partner seeking forgiveness, it means showing consistent effort and understanding that trust cannot be restored overnight. Impatience or pressure to "move on" can undermine the process and create further emotional distance.

Another key component of rebuilding trust is demonstrating reliability. Trust is built through consistent, positive actions over time. This might involve small gestures, like showing up when you say you will, or larger commitments, like actively participating in couples counseling or making lifestyle changes to address underlying issues. Each act of reliability reinforces the idea that the relationship is a safe and stable space, gradually rebuilding the emotional foundation.

Forgiveness is an essential but often misunderstood part of rebuilding trust. Forgiveness doesn't mean forgetting the hurt or condoning the breach—it means choosing to let go of resentment and allowing space for healing. It's a process that requires both partners to work through their emotions and reach a place of mutual understanding. For the betrayed partner, forgiveness can be an act of self-liberation, releasing the emotional burden of anger and pain. For the partner seeking forgiveness, it's an opportunity to demonstrate genuine remorse and a commitment to growth.

Communication plays a central role in this journey. Regular, honest conversations about progress, feelings, and expectations help ensure that both partners remain aligned. These conversations don't need to be formal or structured; sometimes, simply checking in with each other—asking questions like, "How are you feeling about where we're at?" or "What can I do to support you right now?"—can create opportunities for connection and reassurance.

In some cases, rebuilding trust may require professional support. A counselor or therapist can provide guidance, tools, and a neutral space for partners to work through their emotions and challenges. Professional support is particularly valuable for addressing deeper wounds or recurring patterns that may be difficult to resolve independently. Seeking help is not a sign of weakness; it's a demonstration of commitment to the relationship and a willingness to invest in its future.

Rebuilding trust is a journey that requires vulnerability, effort, and perseverance from both partners. It's not an easy process, but it can lead to a stronger, more resilient relationship. When couples commit to rebuilding trust, they create a foundation that not only repairs the past but also strengthens their bond for the future. Through honesty, accountability, and a shared willingness to grow, even the most broken trust can be mended, transforming a painful chapter into a story of healing and renewal.

Embracing Change and Growth

Change is an inevitable part of life, and relationships are no exception. Over time, individuals evolve, circumstances shift, and the dynamics of a partnership transform. While these changes can be challenging, they also present opportunities for growth—both as individuals and as a couple. Embracing change with openness, curiosity, and a shared commitment to adaptation is a hallmark of resilient relationships. It's not about resisting the tides of change but learning to navigate them together, allowing your bond to grow stronger in the process.

One of the most important aspects of embracing change is recognizing that personal growth doesn't stop when you enter a relationship. Each partner is an individual with their own dreams, ambitions, and experiences that continue to shape them over time. Supporting each other's personal growth is essential for maintaining a healthy and dynamic relationship. For instance, if one partner decides to pursue a career shift or a new educational opportunity, the other can offer encouragement and practical support, even if the change disrupts established routines. This willingness to grow together rather than apart creates a sense of partnership that can weather life's uncertainties.

Change also often comes in the form of external circumstances, such as relocations, career transitions, or shifts in family dynamics. These changes can disrupt the equilibrium of a relationship, but they also provide opportunities to explore new ways of connecting and collaborating. For example, a couple facing a move to a new city might use the transition as an opportunity to discover shared interests, like exploring local landmarks or building new social connections. By reframing change as an adventure rather than a threat, couples can foster a sense of excitement and shared purpose.

Adapting to change requires effective communication. Partners need to share their thoughts, concerns, and expectations openly to ensure they're aligned. This might involve discussing how a change will impact each person individually as well as the relationship as a whole. For instance, when welcoming a new baby into the family, couples might discuss how to divide responsibilities, manage stress, and maintain their connection amidst the demands of parenting. These conversations help prevent misunderstandings and ensure that both partners feel heard and supported.

Flexibility is another key component of embracing change. No matter how carefully plans are made, unexpected challenges and opportunities will arise. Being able to adjust expectations and adapt to new realities is essential for maintaining harmony. For example, if one partner's work schedule changes unexpectedly, the other might take on additional responsibilities at home or suggest creative ways to spend quality time together. This flexibility not only helps the relationship navigate change but also demonstrates a willingness to prioritize the partnership over rigid expectations.

Another critical aspect of navigating change is cultivating a growth mindset. Couples who view challenges as opportunities for learning and improvement are better equipped to adapt and thrive. For instance, a couple facing financial difficulties might use the experience to reevaluate their spending habits, set new financial goals, and strengthen their teamwork in managing resources. This proactive approach turns adversity into an opportunity for growth, reinforcing the relationship's resilience.

While adapting to change is important, it's equally essential to honor the relationship's foundation. Maintaining shared traditions, values, and rituals provides a sense of stability amidst the flux of life. For example, even during a period of upheaval, a couple might prioritize their tradition of a weekly date night as a way to stay connected. These rituals act as anchors, grounding the relationship in its shared history while allowing room for evolution.

Finally, embracing change requires patience and compassion. Growth, whether individual or relational, takes time, and it's not always a linear process. There may be setbacks, missteps, or moments of doubt along the way. Offering understanding and support to each other during these times is crucial. For example, if one partner struggles with a new responsibility or adjustment, the other might offer reassurance, reminding them that growth is a process and that they're not alone in navigating it.

In the end, embracing change is about viewing your relationship as a living, evolving entity. It's about accepting that growth sometimes requires discomfort and that change, while challenging, can lead to deeper intimacy and connection. By facing change with an open heart and a shared commitment to adaptation, couples can not only survive life's transitions but thrive because of them. The ability to grow together through change is one of the most powerful ways to build a resilient, enduring partnership.

Challenges are an inevitable part of every relationship, but they are not its undoing. Instead, they offer an opportunity to grow closer, deepen understanding, and build a foundation of resilience that strengthens the bond between two people. In this chapter, we've explored how embracing conflict, fostering empathy, and adapting to change can transform difficult moments into stepping stones toward a stronger, more connected partnership.

Understanding the nature of conflict revealed that disagreements are not threats but signals that something needs attention. By addressing the root causes of tension, recognizing emotional triggers, and reframing arguments as opportunities for collaboration, couples can turn friction into progress. Conflict, when approached with care, becomes a tool for growth rather than a source of division.

Building emotional resilience showed us that relationships thrive when both partners cultivate self-awareness, practice emotional regulation, and support one another through life's challenges. Resilience isn't about avoiding difficulties—it's about facing them with a growth mindset and the belief that love is worth the effort. These practices create a relationship that doesn't just survive adversity but grows stronger because of it.

The power of empathy and active listening reminded us of the transformative impact of truly hearing and understanding one another. When partners feel seen and validated, even during moments of conflict, it fosters a sense of safety and connection that is the cornerstone of lasting love. Active listening and empathy are acts of love that bridge gaps, de-escalate tension, and create an environment where vulnerability can flourish.

Teamwork and shared problem-solving highlighted the importance of approaching challenges as a united front. By shifting from "me" and "you" to "us," couples can tackle obstacles with a sense of partnership and mutual respect. Working together not only resolves immediate issues but also reinforces the idea that the relationship is a shared endeavor, built on trust, cooperation, and shared goals.

Rebuilding trust after challenges showed us that even the most significant breaches can be repaired with honesty, accountability, and consistent effort. Trust is not rebuilt in a single moment but through a series of intentional actions that demonstrate commitment and care. This process of repair can lead to a relationship that is even stronger than before, proving that love can endure and grow through even the most trying times.

Finally, embracing change and growth emphasized the importance of adapting to life's inevitable transitions while maintaining the core values and traditions that anchor a relationship. Change is not something to fear but a natural part of the journey. Couples who face change with flexibility, curiosity, and a shared commitment to growth create a partnership that evolves and thrives over time.

Taken together, these elements form a comprehensive roadmap for navigating challenges and building resilience in relationships. Each strategy reinforces the idea that love is not a static state but a dynamic, ever-evolving journey that requires intention, effort, and care. Challenges, rather than weakening a relationship, can serve as opportunities to strengthen the bond and reaffirm the commitment that brought two people together.

As we move forward to the next chapter, which explores how relationships can fuel personal growth and self-discovery, remember that every difficulty faced together is a step toward something greater. The ability to navigate challenges with empathy, resilience, and teamwork is not just a testament to the strength of your relationship—it's a celebration of the enduring power of love to transform, heal, and inspire.

Personal Growth Through Dating

Dating isn't just about finding the right partner—it's also a profound journey of self-discovery and personal growth. Every relationship, whether fleeting or enduring, teaches us something about who we are, what we value, and how we connect with others. Chapter 7 explores how dating can be a powerful tool for individual growth, helping you to develop emotional intelligence, resilience, and a deeper understanding of yourself.

When approached with intentionality, dating becomes a mirror, reflecting your strengths, vulnerabilities, and areas for improvement. It challenges you to communicate more effectively, navigate complex emotions, and expand your perspective. In this chapter, we'll explore how the dating experience can foster self-awareness, build confidence, and inspire personal evolution. By the end, you'll see that the journey of dating isn't just about finding love—it's also about becoming the best version of yourself.

Emotional intelligence is the cornerstone of these skills, empowering you to communicate effectively, manage challenges, and deepen your relationships. Before we delve into how dating can sharpen your emotional intelligence, let's explore why this skill is essential not only for romantic success but for personal growth as a whole.

Developing Emotional Intelligence

Emotional intelligence is one of the most valuable skills you can cultivate, and dating provides countless opportunities to develop it. At its core, emotional intelligence is the ability to understand and manage your own emotions while also empathizing with and responding to the emotions of others. It encompasses self-awareness, empathy, emotional regulation, and social skills—all essential ingredients for meaningful connections. Through dating, you're constantly engaging in situations that challenge you to practice these skills, making it a powerful environment for emotional growth.

Self-awareness is often the first step in developing emotional intelligence. Dating requires you to reflect on your own feelings, motivations, and patterns. For instance, you might notice that you feel anxious before a first date or defensive during a disagreement. Instead of brushing these feelings aside, self-awareness invites you to examine them: Why do I feel this way? Is it tied to past experiences or unmet expectations? By identifying your emotional triggers, you can approach dating with greater clarity and understanding of yourself.

This self-awareness extends to understanding your needs and boundaries. What do you truly value in a partner? What behaviors or dynamics make you feel uncomfortable or unsupported? Dating forces you to confront these questions, helping you define what you want and what you're willing to compromise on. For example, if you consistently find yourself drawn to people who are emotionally unavailable, recognizing this pattern can empower you to make different choices that align with your emotional needs.

Empathy, another pillar of emotional intelligence, is developed as you navigate the complexities of connecting with another person. Every date is an opportunity to step into someone else's world—to listen to their stories, understand their perspective, and appreciate their emotions. For example, when your date shares a stressful experience, responding with genuine curiosity and compassion strengthens the connection while honing your ability to tune into others' feelings. Empathy is the bridge that transforms surface-level interactions into meaningful exchanges.

Emotional regulation is equally important in dating, as it helps you manage your responses during emotionally charged situations. Dating can be a rollercoaster of emotions—excitement, nervousness, disappointment, and even frustration. How you handle these emotions says a lot about your emotional intelligence. For instance, if a date cancels last minute, you might initially feel hurt or rejected. Emotional regulation allows you to pause, process the situation, and respond thoughtfully rather than reacting impulsively. This skill not only helps you maintain your composure but also fosters healthier interactions with others.

Dating also challenges you to navigate social dynamics and refine your interpersonal skills. From interpreting nonverbal cues to balancing humor and vulnerability, every interaction teaches you something new about effective communication. For example, you might learn how to read subtle signs of interest or disengagement, adjust your approach based on your date's comfort level, or gracefully navigate awkward moments. These experiences enhance your ability to build rapport, resolve misunderstandings, and create a sense of emotional safety.

As you develop emotional intelligence, you'll also notice its impact on your relationships beyond dating. Improved self-awareness helps you articulate your feelings and needs more clearly, while empathy allows you to understand and support others more deeply. Emotional regulation prevents conflicts from escalating, and strong social skills make it easier to connect with friends, family, and colleagues. In this way, dating becomes a training ground for building emotional intelligence that benefits every area of your life.

Ultimately, dating is not just about finding the right person—it's about becoming the best version of yourself. By embracing the opportunities for emotional growth that dating provides, you'll not only improve your relationships but also deepen your understanding of who you are and what you bring to the table. Emotional intelligence is a skill that evolves over time, and with every interaction, you're shaping yourself into a more self-aware, empathetic, and emotionally resilient individual.

Building Resilience Through Rejection and Challenges

Dating, for all its excitement and potential, comes with its fair share of challenges. Rejection, miscommunication, unmet expectations, and moments of vulnerability are part of the journey, and while these experiences can be difficult, they also offer invaluable lessons in resilience. Building resilience through dating is about learning to see these challenges not as failures but as opportunities to grow stronger, both emotionally and mentally. The ability to bounce back from setbacks and navigate difficulties with grace is a skill that benefits not only your romantic life but every aspect of your personal growth.

Rejection is one of the most common and often most painful aspects of dating. Whether it's a one-sided crush, a breakup, or a lack of chemistry after a promising first date, rejection can feel deeply personal. However, resilience begins with reframing these experiences. Instead of internalizing rejection as a reflection of your worth, consider it as valuable feedback about compatibility. A date that doesn't work out isn't an indictment of your character; it's a step closer to finding someone who truly aligns with you. Viewing rejection through this lens transforms it from a source of pain into a tool for self-awareness and redirection.

Resilience also involves cultivating a growth mindset—the belief that every challenge holds the potential for learning and improvement. For example, if a relationship ends due to communication issues, reflecting on what went wrong and what you could do differently next time allows you to grow from the experience. This mindset shifts the focus from blame or self-pity to empowerment, reminding you that setbacks are temporary and part of a larger journey toward connection and self-discovery.

Another key to building resilience is developing emotional regulation. Dating can be a rollercoaster of highs and lows, and learning to navigate these fluctuations with steadiness is essential. Imagine receiving a message that someone you were excited about isn't interested in pursuing things further. It's natural to feel disappointment, but resilience teaches you to acknowledge those emotions without letting them define your self-worth. Techniques like deep breathing, journaling, or talking with a trusted friend can help you process your feelings and move forward with clarity and confidence.

Challenges in dating also teach you how to navigate uncertainty and build patience. In a world of instant gratification, waiting for the right connection can be frustrating. Resilience involves embracing this uncertainty and trusting the process, knowing that meaningful relationships take time to develop. It's about staying open to possibilities without rushing or settling for something that doesn't truly align with your values and needs.

Another aspect of resilience is the ability to learn from patterns in your dating experiences. For example, if you find yourself repeatedly drawn to partners who are emotionally unavailable, reflecting on why this dynamic appeals to you can provide valuable insights. Perhaps it highlights an area of growth, such as setting healthier boundaries or recognizing your own emotional needs. By addressing these patterns with self-compassion and curiosity, you break cycles that no longer serve you, paving the way for healthier connections.

Building resilience also means celebrating progress, even when the outcomes aren't perfect. Every step you take—whether it's initiating a conversation, going on a first date, or ending a relationship that no longer serves you—represents growth. Recognizing and honoring these milestones reinforces the idea that you're continually evolving, no matter the challenges you face.

Resilience doesn't mean avoiding pain or pretending everything is fine when it's not. Instead, it's about cultivating the strength to face difficulties head-on, process your emotions, and emerge stronger on the other side. By building this skill through dating, you prepare yourself not only for romantic relationships but also for life's broader challenges. You learn to trust your ability to adapt, grow, and thrive, even when things don't go as planned.

In the end, dating is as much about discovering your own resilience as it is about finding a partner. Each experience—whether joyful or difficult—adds to your understanding of who you are and what you're capable of. Resilience transforms rejection and challenges into stepping stones, helping you navigate the journey of dating with confidence, self-compassion, and hope for what lies ahead.

Discovering and Honoring Your Values

One of the most transformative aspects of dating is the opportunity it provides to discover and clarify your personal values. Every interaction, whether it results in a lasting relationship or not, sheds light on what truly matters to you in a partner and in life. By reflecting on these experiences, you begin to understand not only what you want but also what you need to feel fulfilled and supported. Honoring your values is about aligning your choices with your authentic self and building connections that resonate with your deepest priorities.

Dating often acts as a mirror, revealing your non-negotiables and uncovering the qualities you seek in a relationship. For instance, after dating someone whose lifestyle felt incompatible with yours—perhaps they prioritized spontaneity while you value structure—you might realize the importance of shared goals and habits. These realizations aren't about judging others but about recognizing what aligns with your own sense of purpose and happiness. Each date becomes an opportunity to refine your understanding of what you want from a partnership.

Equally important is the process of recognizing red flags and celebrating green flags in your dating experiences. Red flags—such as dishonesty, lack of respect, or mismatched priorities—serve as signals that a connection might not be sustainable. On the other hand, green flags, like kindness, active listening, and shared values, highlight the qualities that foster healthy, fulfilling relationships. By paying attention to these signs, you empower yourself to make decisions that align with your values and avoid compromising on what truly matters to you.

Discovering your values through dating also involves reflecting on past relationships and their impact on your growth. What worked well, and what didn't? For example, a relationship where communication was a struggle might lead you to value openness and transparency more deeply in future connections. Alternatively, a partner who supported your ambitions might help you recognize the importance of shared encouragement and mutual respect. These lessons allow you to approach new relationships with greater clarity and intention.

Honoring your values also means setting boundaries that protect your emotional well-being. Boundaries are not about keeping others out but about creating a space where you feel respected, safe, and empowered. For instance, if you value honesty, you might set a boundary around how you handle dishonesty in a relationship, ensuring that you address it openly and directly. These boundaries help you maintain alignment with your values, even in the face of challenges or compromises.

Dating is also a powerful tool for uncovering hidden or evolving values. Sometimes, the qualities you thought were essential may shift as you gain more experience and insight. For example, you might have once prioritized a partner's professional success, only to realize that emotional availability and shared quality time matter more to you. Dating helps you uncover these evolving priorities, allowing you to build connections that reflect your current self rather than outdated expectations.

Another key aspect of discovering your values is learning to articulate them effectively. Once you've identified what's important to you, communicating these values to potential partners becomes essential. For example, if you value personal growth, you might share your enthusiasm for self-improvement during a conversation, gauging whether your date shares similar aspirations. Clear communication about your values not only helps you find compatible partners but also establishes a foundation of honesty and mutual understanding.

Honoring your values through dating is also an act of self-respect. When you align your actions with what matters most to you, you send a powerful message to yourself and others about your worth and integrity. For instance, choosing to walk away from a relationship that doesn't align with your values—no matter how difficult—reinforces your commitment to living authentically.

This self-respect becomes a cornerstone of your confidence and sets the tone for future relationships.

Ultimately, discovering and honoring your values is a journey of self-discovery that extends far beyond dating. It shapes the way you approach life, relationships, and personal growth. By staying true to your values, you not only attract connections that align with your authentic self but also create a foundation for a relationship that is both meaningful and enduring.

Enhancing Communication Skills

Effective communication is the lifeblood of any healthy relationship, and dating offers countless opportunities to develop and refine these essential skills. From navigating first impressions to resolving misunderstandings, every interaction is a chance to practice active listening, articulate your thoughts clearly, and engage in meaningful dialogue. The ability to communicate well not only strengthens romantic connections but also enriches every other aspect of your life, from friendships to professional relationships.

One of the first lessons dating teaches about communication is the importance of clarity. Ambiguity can lead to misunderstandings, misaligned expectations, and frustration for both parties. For example, if you're unsure about your intentions—whether you're looking for a casual connection or a long-term relationship—it's easy to send mixed signals that confuse your date. Being upfront and honest about your goals, preferences, and feelings establishes a foundation of trust and avoids unnecessary tension. Clear communication doesn't mean sharing every detail immediately but finding the right balance between honesty and pacing.

Listening is another critical aspect of communication that dating helps you hone. It's not enough to hear what someone says—you must listen actively, with curiosity and empathy. This means giving your full attention, asking thoughtful questions, and reflecting on what your date shares. For example, if your partner mentions they've had a stressful week, you might respond with, "That sounds overwhelming. What's been the toughest part for you?" This kind of engagement not only deepens the connection but also shows that you value their experiences and emotions.

Navigating disagreements is another area where dating enhances communication skills. Misunderstandings and differences are inevitable, but how you handle them can make or break a connection. Dating teaches you to approach conflicts with patience and an open mind, focusing on resolution rather than blame. For instance, instead of saying, "You're always late, and it's disrespectful," you might say, "I feel unimportant when our plans don't start on time. Can we talk about how we can avoid that in the future?" This approach shifts the focus from accusation to collaboration, fostering a healthier dynamic.

Vulnerability is another essential element of communication that dating encourages you to explore. Sharing your thoughts, feelings, and fears requires courage, especially in the early stages of a relationship. Vulnerability doesn't mean oversharing but finding moments to let your guard down and invite deeper connection. For example, admitting that you're nervous before a date or expressing how much you enjoyed the time together can create an authentic bond. Vulnerability builds trust, signaling that you're invested in the connection and willing to take emotional risks.

Dating also highlights the importance of nonverbal communication. Body language, tone of voice, and eye contact often speak louder than words, shaping the way your messages are received. For example, maintaining eye contact and smiling during a conversation signals interest and attentiveness, while crossing your arms or checking your phone might unintentionally convey disinterest. Becoming aware of your nonverbal cues—and learning to read those of your date—helps you create an atmosphere of openness and respect.

Another valuable communication skill dating teaches is how to address misaligned expectations. No two people approach dating with identical assumptions, and these differences can lead to confusion if left unaddressed. For instance, one person might interpret frequent texting as a sign of serious interest, while the other sees it as casual conversation. Openly discussing your expectations—such as how often you'd like to communicate or what you're looking for in a relationship—prevents misunderstandings and ensures that both partners are on the same page.

As you develop your communication skills through dating, you'll also notice their impact beyond romantic relationships. Improved clarity, active listening, and conflict resolution make it easier to connect with others in every area of your life. These skills empower you to build stronger friendships, navigate workplace dynamics, and approach family interactions with greater empathy and understanding.

Ultimately, dating is a masterclass in communication. Each conversation, question, and shared experience sharpens your ability to connect with others authentically and effectively. By embracing these opportunities for growth, you not only strengthen your relationships but also enhance your ability to express yourself and understand others. Communication is the bridge that turns acquaintances into partners, misunderstandings into solutions, and fleeting moments into lasting connections.

Expanding Your Comfort Zone

Dating is one of life's most effective ways to nudge you out of your comfort zone. It challenges you to meet new people, embrace unfamiliar situations, and confront your own fears and insecurities. While stepping outside your comfort zone can feel intimidating, it's also where growth happens. Each new experience broadens your perspective, builds your confidence, and opens the door to possibilities you might never have considered before.

At its core, dating pushes you to engage with the unknown. Whether it's striking up a conversation with someone you just met, trying a new activity for a date, or navigating cultural or lifestyle differences, these moments force you to stretch beyond what feels safe and familiar. For example, agreeing to go rock climbing on a date when you've never attempted it before might feel daunting, but it also provides an opportunity to challenge yourself and discover new strengths. These experiences help you grow not only as a partner but also as an individual.

One of the most significant ways dating expands your comfort zone is by encouraging you to face vulnerability. Putting yourself out there, especially in the face of potential rejection, requires courage and self-assurance. The nervousness before a first date or the hesitation in sharing something personal is a natural part of the process. Overcoming these moments builds emotional resilience and teaches you to trust in your own worth, regardless of the outcome.

Dating also helps you explore and appreciate diversity. Meeting people from different backgrounds, cultures, and perspectives enriches your understanding of the world. For example, dating someone who grew up in a different country might introduce you to new traditions, cuisines, or ways of thinking. These interactions broaden your worldview, fostering empathy and adaptability while challenging preconceived notions. Expanding your social circle through dating is not just about finding a partner—it's about becoming a more open and curious individual.

Another way dating pushes you out of your comfort zone is by encouraging you to try new activities and environments. Dates often involve experiences you might not have pursued on your own, like visiting a new art exhibit, hiking an unfamiliar trail, or attending a dance class. These activities not only create opportunities for connection but also add to your personal repertoire of interests and skills. Over time, the willingness to embrace novelty becomes a habit, making you more adventurous and open to change in other areas of life.

Expanding your comfort zone through dating also involves confronting and challenging your fears. For instance, if you've experienced a painful breakup in the past, the idea of opening your heart to someone new might feel overwhelming. But each step you take—whether it's agreeing to meet someone for coffee or joining a dating app—gradually helps you rebuild trust in yourself and in the process of connection. Facing these fears head-on empowers you to move forward with confidence and optimism.

Dating can also challenge you to rethink your preferences and expectations. While it's important to know your values and non-negotiables, remaining too rigid in your criteria can limit your opportunities for connection. For example, you might initially be hesitant to date someone whose hobbies or lifestyle differ from your own, only to discover that those differences complement and enrich your relationship. By stepping outside your usual "type," you open yourself to the possibility of unexpected connections that can teach you more about yourself and what you truly value.

Over time, expanding your comfort zone through dating has a ripple effect on other areas of your life. The confidence you gain from trying new things and navigating unfamiliar situations translates into greater self-assurance in your career, friendships, and personal pursuits. You become more willing to take risks, embrace change, and step into the unknown with curiosity and courage.

Ultimately, dating is about growth, and growth rarely happens without discomfort. By embracing the challenges and uncertainties that come with stepping outside your comfort zone, you not only increase your chances of finding meaningful connections but also become a more adaptable, confident, and fulfilled individual. The willingness to stretch beyond your limits is a testament to your resilience and your belief in the possibilities that lie ahead.

Fostering Self-Love and Confidence

One of the most profound outcomes of dating is the opportunity it provides to foster self-love and build confidence. While the process of forming connections with others often highlights shared interests and compatibility, it also brings into focus your relationship with yourself. Self-love is the foundation upon which all healthy relationships are built, and dating offers countless chances to nurture that foundation, reminding you of your worth, setting boundaries that reflect your needs, and cultivating confidence in who you are.

At its core, self-love begins with self-awareness. Dating encourages you to reflect on what you truly want, both in a partner and in a relationship. This process often reveals more about your own values, needs, and aspirations. For instance, after dating someone who didn't respect your time or emotional energy, you may realize the importance of setting boundaries and prioritizing your well-being. Recognizing these lessons and acting on them is an act of self-love, reaffirming that your happiness and growth are non-negotiable.

Boundaries play a vital role in fostering self-love and confidence. When you set and maintain healthy boundaries, you communicate to yourself and others that you value your time, energy, and emotional well-being. For example, if you find yourself in a relationship where your needs are consistently overlooked, self-love might mean having the courage to address the imbalance—or even walk away if necessary. These actions reinforce your sense of self-worth, demonstrating that you are deserving of respect and care.

Dating also provides a platform for celebrating your individuality. Each connection and conversation is an opportunity to showcase your unique qualities and passions. Whether it's sharing your favorite hobby, discussing your dreams, or expressing your sense of humor, these moments allow you to embrace and affirm who you are. The more you lean into your authenticity, the more confident you become in your ability to connect with others on a genuine level.

Rejection, while often painful, is another avenue through which dating fosters self-love and resilience. Being turned down or experiencing a breakup can initially feel like a blow to your confidence, but it also offers an opportunity to practice self-compassion. Instead of internalizing rejection as a reflection of your worth, self-love encourages you to view it as a natural part of the journey—one that redirects you toward more fulfilling opportunities. Each time you choose to nurture yourself through difficult moments, you strengthen your confidence and emotional resilience.

Self-love is also about prioritizing self-care, especially during the ups and downs of dating. It's easy to become consumed by the process, focusing solely on pleasing others or meeting external expectations. However, making time for yourself—whether through journaling, meditation, hobbies, or simply resting—ensures that you stay grounded and connected to your own needs. This balance between seeking connection and nurturing your individuality is key to maintaining both your confidence and your sense of self-worth.

Confidence, like self-love, is cultivated through experience. Each positive interaction, shared laugh, and meaningful conversation reinforces your belief in your ability to connect with others. Even challenging moments, like navigating an awkward first date or overcoming shyness, contribute to your confidence by showing you that you can handle uncertainty and grow from it. Over time, these experiences build a sense of assurance that extends beyond dating, influencing every aspect of your life.

Fostering self-love and confidence also involves recognizing and celebrating your progress. Reflecting on how far you've come—whether it's overcoming past insecurities, embracing vulnerability, or learning to articulate your needs—reinforces your sense of growth and achievement. For example, you might look back on a time when you hesitated to voice your boundaries and feel proud of how confidently you now express them. These moments of reflection are powerful reminders of your resilience and self-worth.

Ultimately, self-love and confidence are not destinations but ongoing practices. Dating provides a dynamic space to nurture these qualities, challenging you to honor your worth, embrace your authenticity, and grow into the person you aspire to be. By fostering a strong relationship with yourself, you create the foundation for deeper, healthier connections with others. The journey begins with you—and every step you take toward self-love and confidence is a step toward a more fulfilling and meaningful life.

Dating is more than just a pathway to finding love—it's a journey of profound personal growth. Each experience, whether joyful or challenging, offers an opportunity to learn, adapt, and evolve into the best version of yourself. By engaging with the process intentionally, you discover not only what you seek in a partner but also what you bring to the table as an individual. Through emotional intelligence, resilience, communication, and self-love, dating becomes a mirror reflecting your strengths, vulnerabilities, and potential.

This chapter explored how dating sharpens emotional intelligence, teaching you to navigate your own emotions while empathizing with others. It showed how resilience, cultivated through rejection and challenges, transforms setbacks into stepping stones toward greater self-awareness and confidence. It demonstrated the importance of discovering and honoring your values, ensuring that your relationships align with your authentic self.

We also examined how dating enhances communication skills, fostering better listening, self-expression, and conflict resolution. The willingness to expand your comfort zone opens doors to new experiences, perspectives, and personal growth, while fostering self-love and confidence reinforces your ability to set boundaries, celebrate your individuality, and embrace vulnerability.

Taken together, these lessons reveal that dating is not merely about finding the right person—it's about becoming the right person. The process encourages you to cultivate qualities that enhance every aspect of your life, from your career to your friendships to your relationship with yourself.

The personal growth you experience through dating lays the foundation for deeper, healthier connections, preparing you not only for romantic success but for a more fulfilling and meaningful life overall.

As we move into the next chapter, which delves into the role of adventure and thrill in relationships, remember that personal growth is a lifelong journey. Each date, each conversation, and each moment of vulnerability is an opportunity to explore new facets of yourself and your relationships. The more you invest in your own growth, the more richly you will experience the world around you—and the more ready you'll be to embrace the adventures that lie ahead.

The Role of Adventure and Thrill

Relationships thrive on connection, but they truly come alive through moments of adventure and thrill. These shared experiences ignite excitement, create vivid memories, and deepen emotional bonds in ways that routine interactions often cannot. Adventure doesn't have to mean scaling mountains or skydiving; it's about stepping out of the familiar and embracing activities that bring novelty, joy, and a sense of accomplishment. Whether it's exploring a new city, trying an unconventional activity, or simply breaking out of a routine, adventure breathes fresh energy into a relationship, keeping it dynamic and fulfilling.

What makes certain moments with your partner unforgettable? Often, it's the thrill of experiencing something new together—the rush of adrenaline, the shared laughter in the face of unexpected challenges, or the quiet awe of discovering something for the first time. These aren't just fleeting joys; they leave a lasting imprint, shaping the story of your relationship. But what is it about adventure that makes it such a powerful force for connection? This chapter delves into the science behind shared experiences, exploring how they spark passion, foster trust, and strengthen bonds. Let's begin with the fascinating connection between adventure and emotional bonding.

The Science of Adventure and Bonding

Adventure isn't just exciting—it's scientifically proven to strengthen relationships. When couples engage in activities that involve novelty, adrenaline, or even a touch of risk, their brains release powerful neurochemicals like dopamine and oxytocin. These chemicals are responsible for feelings of pleasure, connection, and trust, creating an emotional high that deepens bonds. Understanding the psychology behind adventure and its impact on relationships can help couples tap into this dynamic to build stronger, more vibrant connections.

At the core of this phenomenon is the concept of arousal transfer. This psychological principle suggests that heightened emotional states—like the adrenaline rush from trying something thrilling—can amplify feelings of attraction and connection. For example, a couple who goes zip-lining together might feel exhilarated by the activity itself, but that excitement often carries over into their perception of each other. The shared adrenaline creates a sense of closeness, making the experience both exciting and bonding.

Adventure also taps into the brain's reward system by introducing novelty. Over time, relationships can fall into routines that, while comforting, may lack the spark of excitement. Novel experiences stimulate the release of dopamine, the "feel-good" neurotransmitter associated with pleasure and motivation. When couples break out of their routines and try something new—whether it's taking a dance class, exploring a new city, or attempting a daring activity—they reignite the excitement that often characterizes the early stages of a relationship. These shared experiences create a sense of discovery, not just of the activity but of each other, fostering a renewed sense of curiosity and attraction.

Shared adventures also create emotional anchors—memories tied to heightened emotions that become cherished parts of a couple's history. The psychology of memory tells us that experiences associated with strong emotions are more likely to be vividly remembered. For instance, a couple who hikes to a breathtaking mountaintop may find that the view becomes a symbolic reminder of their teamwork, perseverance, and shared joy. These memories serve as touchstones that couples can revisit, reinforcing their bond over time.

Moreover, adventure strengthens trust. Engaging in thrilling or challenging activities often requires partners to rely on one another, whether it's spotting each other on a climbing wall or navigating unfamiliar terrain together. This reliance fosters a sense of teamwork and mutual support, building trust in both big and small ways. Even minor adventures, like trying a new restaurant or solving an escape room challenge, create opportunities for collaboration and shared problem-solving.

It's important to note that adventure doesn't have to mean extreme sports or extravagant plans. The science of bonding through novelty and excitement applies to a wide range of activities, from the daring to the simple. For some couples, adventure might mean kayaking through rapids; for others, it could be as low-key as trying a new cuisine or attending an improv class. The key is stepping outside of the familiar and embracing the unknown together.

Adventure also provides a healthy outlet for managing stress in a relationship. Life's challenges can sometimes create tension between partners, but shared adventures offer a way to channel that energy into something positive. For example, a couple dealing with a particularly stressful period might find relief and connection in planning a weekend getaway or engaging in a fun physical activity like rock climbing. These shared moments not only alleviate stress but also remind couples of the joy they bring to each other's lives.

Ultimately, the science of adventure and bonding reveals that excitement and connection are deeply intertwined. By seeking out new experiences and embracing moments of thrill, couples can not only strengthen their relationships but also create a shared narrative filled with joy, discovery, and lasting memories. Adventure isn't just about the activity itself—it's about the way it brings two people closer together, creating a relationship that feels dynamic, engaging, and full of life.

Micro-Adventures: Thrills in Everyday Life

Adventure doesn't always require a plane ticket or elaborate planning. Some of the most meaningful and exciting experiences can be found in the simplicity of everyday life. Micro-adventures are small, accessible, and often spontaneous activities that infuse relationships with a sense of novelty and fun. These moments, though seemingly ordinary, have the power to strengthen bonds, break up routines, and bring joy into a partnership.

At its core, a micro-adventure is about looking at the familiar with fresh eyes. It's not about the grandeur of the activity but the shared excitement it creates. For example, a couple might decide to explore a neighborhood they've never visited, sampling food from local food trucks or discovering quirky shops. Another might turn an evening walk into a mini scavenger hunt, finding and sharing little treasures along the way. These experiences don't require extensive planning or expense but still offer the thrill of discovery and connection.

Spontaneity is a key element of micro-adventures. By saying yes to unexpected opportunities or breaking out of established routines, couples invite a sense of playfulness and creativity into their relationship. For instance, choosing to drive without a set destination, picking a restaurant at random, or taking an impromptu dance lesson injects an element of surprise and delight into the day. These moments of spontaneity remind couples that adventure doesn't have to be far-reaching to feel exhilarating.

Micro-adventures also help couples reconnect in the midst of busy lives. It's easy for work, responsibilities, and daily routines to overshadow the need for quality time. Small adventures—like trying a new recipe together, building a blanket fort for a movie night, or attending a local festival—create pockets of joy that strengthen the bond between partners. These shared activities are particularly valuable for couples who may not have the time or resources for grand gestures but still want to keep their relationship dynamic and engaging.

The beauty of micro-adventures lies in their accessibility. They allow couples to tap into the spirit of adventure without needing to leave their city, spend a lot of money, or make extensive plans. For example, hiking a nearby trail, visiting a museum on a whim, or stargazing in the backyard can transform an ordinary day into something special. These small, shared experiences create lasting memories and reinforce the idea that adventure is a state of mind rather than a specific activity.

Another benefit of micro-adventures is the opportunity they provide for emotional intimacy. Trying something new together often requires teamwork, communication, and trust—whether it's navigating a new biking route or building a DIY project at home. These shared efforts strengthen the emotional connection between partners, reminding them that they're a team capable of tackling both fun challenges and life's larger obstacles.

Micro-adventures also offer a chance to inject humor and lightheartedness into a relationship. The unpredictable nature of these experiences often leads to funny mishaps or unexpected surprises, like getting lost on the way to a hidden gem or laughing at each other's attempts at a new skill. These moments of shared laughter create a sense of playfulness that deepens the bond between partners and fosters positive associations in the relationship.

In the end, micro-adventures are about making the ordinary extraordinary. They remind couples that adventure isn't defined by the scale of the experience but by the connection, joy, and spontaneity it brings. By embracing small thrills and everyday surprises, couples can infuse their relationship with vitality and create a shared narrative filled with moments of joy, discovery, and togetherness.

Facing Challenges Together

Adventure isn't just about excitement and fun—it's also about embracing challenges that test your limits and deepen your partnership. When couples face obstacles together, they build trust, resilience, and a sense of teamwork that strengthens their bond. From physical challenges like tackling a difficult hike to emotional ones like overcoming shared fears, navigating these moments as a team fosters growth and creates a foundation for a lasting connection.

One of the most profound aspects of facing challenges together is the way it builds trust. When you rely on your partner to guide you through a tough situation—whether it's spotting you during a rock-climbing session or offering encouragement during a daunting presentation—you develop a deeper belief in their dependability. This trust extends beyond the activity itself, reinforcing your confidence in the relationship as a whole. Knowing that your partner has your back, both physically and emotionally, creates a sense of security that is essential for long-term connection.

Overcoming challenges also requires effective communication and problem-solving. For example, imagine a couple trying to navigate a canoe through turbulent waters. Success depends on their ability to communicate clearly, adjust their strategy, and support each other through mistakes. These moments of collaboration teach couples how to work together under pressure, a skill that proves invaluable when facing larger life obstacles. The ability to adapt and problem-solve as a team strengthens the partnership and reinforces the idea that you're in it together.

Shared challenges also create opportunities for vulnerability, an essential ingredient for intimacy. When you step out of your comfort zone, you're forced to confront fears or insecurities that might otherwise remain hidden. For instance, attempting a high ropes course might reveal one partner's fear of heights, while the other's encouragement helps them push through it. These moments of vulnerability not only build trust but also deepen the emotional connection, showing that it's safe to lean on each other during times of uncertainty.

Another powerful aspect of facing challenges together is the sense of accomplishment it brings. Achieving a goal as a team—whether it's completing a tough physical feat, solving a tricky escape room puzzle, or navigating a road trip detour—creates a shared sense of pride and satisfaction. These accomplishments become part of the couple's shared narrative, reinforcing their ability to overcome obstacles together and celebrating their growth as a unit.

It's important to note that challenges don't have to be extreme to be meaningful. Everyday obstacles, like assembling furniture, tackling a DIY home project, or planning a last-minute event, also provide opportunities for teamwork and connection. These smaller challenges help couples build a foundation of trust and resilience that prepares them for larger trials. By navigating even minor hurdles together, partners learn to appreciate each other's strengths and offer support where needed.

Facing challenges together also cultivates a sense of adventure and excitement in the relationship. The adrenaline and focus required to overcome obstacles often mirror the thrill of traditional adventure activities, creating a similar boost in emotional connection. For example, a couple who tackles a difficult hiking trail might feel the same sense of exhilaration and bonding as one who embarks on a more traditional "adventure." These shared highs bring energy and vitality to the relationship.

In the broader context of life, the ability to face challenges together builds resilience, both individually and as a couple. Life is full of unexpected twists and turns, from career changes to family crises, and the skills developed through shared challenges in adventure translate directly to navigating these realities. Couples who have learned to work together during smaller challenges are better equipped to handle life's larger obstacles with grace and unity.

Ultimately, facing challenges together strengthens the emotional and practical foundation of a relationship. It builds trust, fosters collaboration, and deepens intimacy by showing partners what they can achieve when they work as a team. Whether the challenge is big or small, the effort to overcome it together becomes a testament to the strength of the partnership, creating lasting memories and a bond that grows stronger with each shared triumph.

Rekindling Passion Through Novelty

Routine is the silent comfort of long-term relationships, providing stability and predictability, but it can also dull the spark of passion over time. Rekindling that spark doesn't require grand gestures or dramatic changes—it simply calls for novelty. By introducing new experiences, couples can reignite their sense of curiosity and excitement, creating moments that remind them of why they fell in love in the first place. Novelty has a unique power to rejuvenate relationships, infusing them with energy and intimacy that can be sustained over time.

At the heart of novelty's impact is the psychological principle of reward anticipation. When couples try something new together, their brains release dopamine, the same neurotransmitter responsible for the euphoria of falling in love. This chemical boost creates a sense of exhilaration and connection, making the experience not only enjoyable but also deeply bonding. For instance, exploring a new hobby, taking an impromptu road trip, or even changing the setting of a regular date night can recreate the thrill of early romance.

Novelty also encourages couples to see each other in a new light. Trying something unfamiliar—whether it's taking a salsa class or learning a foreign language together—offers a chance to witness your partner's adaptability, creativity, and willingness to embrace challenges. These moments of discovery can reignite admiration and appreciation, reminding you of the qualities that initially drew you to your partner. For example, watching your partner confidently navigate an unexpected twist during an activity can spark a renewed sense of pride and attraction.

Breaking out of routines doesn't have to involve extravagant efforts. Simple shifts, like experimenting with a new recipe, rearranging a familiar space, or swapping a traditional dinner date for a picnic under the stars, can breathe fresh air into a relationship. The key is to step away from the familiar and embrace the element of surprise. These small acts of novelty show your partner that you're invested in keeping the relationship dynamic and exciting, no matter how long you've been together.

Another powerful way to rekindle passion through novelty is by sharing "firsts." First-time experiences have a unique ability to strengthen bonds because they create shared memories that stand out against the backdrop of routine.

Whether it's traveling to a destination you've both dreamed of, trying an extreme sport, or simply visiting a new café in town, these moments create a sense of joint exploration and discovery. They reinforce the idea that there's always more to experience together, keeping the relationship fresh and forward-focused.

Novelty also fosters intimacy by encouraging vulnerability. Trying something new often involves stepping outside your comfort zone, which can create opportunities for mutual support and connection. For instance, if you and your partner decide to attempt a challenging activity like kayaking or painting, the inevitable mistakes and learning curve can lead to laughter, encouragement, and shared triumphs. These moments of vulnerability not only strengthen your bond but also create a safe space for deeper emotional intimacy.

Incorporating novelty into a relationship also helps partners reconnect with their playful sides. Playfulness is often associated with the early stages of romance, but it's a quality that can be cultivated at any stage of a relationship. Sharing a spontaneous dance in the kitchen, joking during an impromptu karaoke session, or embracing the silliness of a themed dress-up date rekindles the joy and lightness that first brought you together. This playfulness keeps the relationship vibrant and reminds both partners that love doesn't always have to be serious—it can be fun, too.

Over time, the cumulative effect of novelty is a relationship that feels dynamic and evolving. Each new experience adds a layer of richness to the shared history of the partnership, creating a sense of adventure that sustains passion and connection. By consistently seeking out ways to surprise and delight each other, couples build a relationship that remains exciting and fulfilling, no matter how many years they've been together.

Ultimately, rekindling passion through novelty is about embracing the idea that love is a journey, not a destination. It's about continuously discovering new ways to connect, grow, and enjoy each other's company. By prioritizing novelty and breaking out of routines, couples can reignite the spark of passion and create a relationship that feels as thrilling as it did at the very beginning.

Adventure and Long-Term Happiness

Adventure isn't just a fleeting thrill—it plays a crucial role in sustaining long-term happiness in relationships. Over time, the initial spark of a partnership can give way to a comfortable routine. While stability is important, the absence of novelty and excitement can lead to stagnation. Incorporating adventure into a relationship helps couples maintain a sense of joy, curiosity, and connection that fuels lasting satisfaction and fulfillment. By balancing the comfort of routine with the thrill of adventure, couples can create a relationship that feels dynamic and ever-evolving.

One of the key ways adventure contributes to long-term happiness is by fostering a sense of shared purpose. When couples engage in exciting or challenging activities together, they work as a team to overcome obstacles and enjoy the rewards of their efforts. For example, planning a trip, tackling a DIY home project, or learning a new skill together creates opportunities for collaboration and mutual support. These shared endeavors remind partners that they're not just individuals—they're part of a dynamic, evolving partnership.

Adventure also helps couples rediscover the joy of play. Playfulness often comes naturally in the early stages of a relationship, but as time goes on, responsibilities and routines can take center stage. Adventure reintroduces that sense of lighthearted fun, allowing couples to laugh, explore, and bond in ways that break up the monotony of daily life. Whether it's a spontaneous road trip, a weekend camping excursion, or simply trying a quirky activity like goat yoga, these playful experiences keep the relationship fresh and invigorating.

Another benefit of adventure is its ability to reignite passion and intimacy. Novel experiences stimulate the release of dopamine, the same neurotransmitter responsible for the euphoric feelings of early love. By continuing to seek out new adventures together, couples can recreate that spark and maintain the excitement that drew them to each other in the first place. For instance, sharing the exhilaration of a hot air balloon ride or the quiet thrill of discovering a hidden beach can create powerful emotional memories that reinforce the bond between partners.

Adventure also encourages couples to embrace growth and change as a natural part of their relationship. Every new experience, whether it's traveling to a foreign country or trying a challenging cooking class, brings with it lessons and insights. These experiences help partners grow individually while strengthening their connection as a team. By embracing the idea that love is a journey rather than a destination, couples can maintain a sense of curiosity and exploration that keeps their relationship dynamic.

Importantly, adventure doesn't have to be grand or expensive to be meaningful. Small adventures, like exploring a new hiking trail, attending a community event, or simply rearranging your living space together, can have just as much impact as larger-scale experiences. The key is the shared sense of discovery and excitement that comes from stepping outside the ordinary. These moments remind couples that adventure is a state of mind, not just an activity.

Balancing adventure with routine is essential for long-term happiness. While routine provides the stability and predictability that relationships need to thrive, too much routine can lead to a sense of stagnation. Adventure acts as a counterbalance, injecting energy and novelty into the partnership. For example, a couple might maintain their tradition of a weekly date night but choose to vary the activity each time—one week trying a new restaurant, the next attending a live music event, and the following week taking a sunset stroll. This balance keeps the relationship grounded while ensuring it remains exciting.

Over time, the shared memories created through adventure become an integral part of the relationship's narrative. These experiences serve as touchstones that couples can look back on with fondness and pride, reinforcing their bond and reminding them of the joy they bring to each other's lives. Whether it's the story of a road trip mishap that turned into a hilarious adventure or the memory of a quiet night stargazing, these moments become part of the couple's shared identity.

Ultimately, adventure and long-term happiness go hand in hand. By embracing new experiences, couples not only keep their relationship vibrant but also deepen their connection and create a lasting sense of fulfillment. Adventure is more than just a break from the routine—it's a way to celebrate the journey of love and partnership, ensuring that the spark never fades and the relationship continues to flourish over time.

Adventure is not just an occasional thrill; it's a cornerstone of a vibrant, lasting relationship. By embracing the spirit of adventure—whether through small, spontaneous moments or grand, daring experiences—couples can infuse their partnership with energy, joy, and resilience. This chapter has explored how adventure strengthens emotional bonds, fosters trust, and rekindles passion, offering a pathway to deeper connection and long-term happiness.

The science of bonding through adventure highlights the transformative power of shared adrenaline, novelty, and excitement. These experiences spark emotions that bring partners closer, creating cherished memories that become the foundation of a shared narrative. Whether it's a daring zip-line ride or a quiet moment of discovery, adventure amplifies the connection between two people, reminding them of the excitement that first brought them together.

Through micro-adventures, couples can rediscover the magic of everyday life. These small, accessible moments—like exploring a new park, trying an unfamiliar recipe, or embarking on a spontaneous road trip—offer opportunities to break free from routine and reconnect. They remind us that adventure doesn't always require grand gestures; it's about the shared spirit of discovery that brings joy and vitality to the relationship.

Facing challenges together is another powerful way that adventure strengthens partnerships. Whether navigating physical obstacles or emotional hurdles, these moments of teamwork and vulnerability build trust and resilience. They show couples that they can rely on each other, not just in moments of ease but in times of uncertainty and growth.

Novelty, as we've seen, is essential for rekindling passion and keeping relationships dynamic. Breaking free from the ordinary to embrace new experiences—big or small—offers a fresh perspective and reinvigorates intimacy. It encourages partners to see each other in new ways, deepening their appreciation and admiration for one another.

Finally, adventure contributes to long-term happiness by balancing routine with novelty. Stability provides the foundation for love to flourish, while adventure injects excitement and spontaneity that keeps the relationship alive. Together, they create a dynamic partnership that evolves with time, sustaining joy and connection through life's inevitable ups and downs.

As we move forward to the next chapter, which delves into the beauty of everyday romance, remember that adventure isn't just an activity; it's a mindset. It's about seeking connection, embracing discovery, and celebrating the journey of love. Whether you're scaling a mountain or sharing a laugh during a quiet evening at home, every adventure you undertake together becomes a part of the story you're writing as a couple—a story that grows richer, deeper, and more fulfilling with each passing chapter.

The Power of Everyday Romance

Romance is often portrayed as grand gestures—sweeping declarations of love, extravagant surprises, and unforgettable moments. While these are undoubtedly memorable, the true strength of a relationship often lies in the quieter, everyday acts of affection. It's in the morning coffee made just the way you like it, the knowing smile shared across a crowded room, or the simple "how was your day?" that's asked with genuine interest. These moments may not feel cinematic, but they are the threads that weave intimacy into daily life.

Everyday romance is about finding joy and connection in the ordinary. It's about showing your partner that they are seen, valued, and cherished—not just on special occasions but in the little moments that fill your days. These acts don't require elaborate planning or grand budgets; they thrive on thoughtfulness and consistency. By cultivating this daily rhythm of affection and care, couples can create a relationship that feels both stable and full of life.

But what is it about small gestures that have such a profound impact? How can something as simple as a handwritten note or a shared laugh strengthen emotional bonds? To understand the transformative power of everyday romance, we must first explore the science behind it—how these small acts shape our relationships and deepen our connections over time.

The Science of Everyday Romance

The secret to lasting relationships isn't found in sporadic grand gestures but in the small, consistent acts of love that happen every day. These seemingly simple moments—like holding hands during a walk or leaving a kind note—hold profound power in strengthening emotional bonds. The science behind everyday romance reveals that it's the regular, thoughtful actions that build trust, foster intimacy, and sustain happiness in a partnership.

At the heart of everyday romance is the concept of emotional deposits, a term coined by psychologist John Gottman. Each kind act, thoughtful word, or moment of attention serves as a deposit into what Gottman calls the "emotional bank account" of a relationship. When these deposits outweigh withdrawals, such as conflicts or moments of neglect, the relationship thrives. Consistent acts of love and thoughtfulness create a reservoir of positive feelings, making couples more resilient in the face of challenges.

Small gestures are also deeply tied to the brain's reward system. Acts of kindness and affection trigger the release of oxytocin, often referred to as the "bonding hormone." This neurochemical fosters feelings of trust, security, and connection, strengthening the emotional bond between partners. For example, a gentle touch, an unexpected compliment, or simply listening attentively can create a surge of oxytocin, reinforcing the sense of closeness and mutual care.

Everyday romance also taps into the psychological principle of reciprocity, where one thoughtful action inspires another. When one partner consistently shows affection and care, it creates a cycle of mutual appreciation and kindness. For instance, a partner who feels valued through small gestures—like having their favorite snack waiting for them after a long day—will naturally feel more inclined to reciprocate, further nurturing the bond.

Beyond the immediate effects, small acts of romance contribute to long-term emotional security. Regular demonstrations of care remind partners that their relationship is a priority, even amid busy schedules and external stressors. For example, taking a moment to text your partner a loving message during a hectic workday or sharing a quiet moment of gratitude at the end of the day reinforces a sense of stability and connection. These small acts of reassurance create a foundation of trust that carries couples through life's challenges.

Moreover, everyday romance has a cumulative effect. While a single kind gesture may feel small in isolation, their consistent presence creates a ripple effect that strengthens the overall quality of the relationship. Over time, these acts build a shared history of love and thoughtfulness, anchoring the relationship in a deep sense of mutual respect and care.

One of the most beautiful aspects of everyday romance is its accessibility. Grand gestures require planning, resources, and time, but small acts of love can be integrated seamlessly into daily life. A smile, a thoughtful question, or a shared laugh costs nothing yet carries immense value. These moments of connection remind partners that romance isn't confined to special occasions—it's a daily practice that keeps the relationship alive and vibrant.

Ultimately, the science of everyday romance underscores a simple yet profound truth: it's the little things that matter most. By showing care and thoughtfulness in small ways, couples create a relationship that feels secure, joyful, and deeply fulfilling. As we delve deeper into the language of small gestures, we'll explore how to recognize and respond to these moments of connection, ensuring that everyday romance becomes a natural and cherished part of your relationship.

The Language of Small Gestures

Romance is often spoken in subtle, unspoken ways. It's in the small gestures that reflect attention, care, and thoughtfulness—expressions of love that go beyond words. Understanding and practicing the language of small gestures is essential for fostering intimacy and keeping a relationship vibrant. These small acts are powerful because they demonstrate effort, consideration, and an understanding of what truly matters to your partner.

At the core of small gestures lies the ability to recognize and respond to your partner's unique needs and preferences. This is where the concept of love languages, popularized by Dr. Gary Chapman, becomes invaluable. Each person has a preferred way of giving and receiving love—whether through words of affirmation, acts of service, physical touch, quality time, or gifts. Understanding your partner's love language allows you to tailor your gestures in a way that resonates most deeply with them. For example, if your partner values quality time, planning an uninterrupted evening together speaks volumes more than a fleeting compliment or a gift.

Small gestures are also opportunities to show that you are paying attention. Remembering details—like their favorite snack, the book they mentioned wanting to read, or how they take their coffee—demonstrates care and attentiveness. These acts may seem insignificant on the surface, but they send a powerful message: "I see you, and you matter to me." For instance, surprising your partner with their favorite treat after a long day shows that you've been listening and are attuned to their needs.

Consistency is another key aspect of the language of small gestures. Grand romantic displays are memorable, but their impact fades without the reinforcement of daily care and thoughtfulness. Simple acts, like saying "good morning" with a smile, checking in during the day, or giving a warm hug before bed, create a rhythm of connection that keeps the relationship steady and secure. These moments become a source of comfort and stability, particularly during stressful times.

Small gestures are also an opportunity to inject creativity and playfulness into your relationship. A note tucked into their bag, a silly inside joke shared at just the right moment, or an impromptu dance in the kitchen can turn ordinary moments into extraordinary ones. These playful acts keep the relationship lighthearted and joyful, reminding both partners that love can be fun and spontaneous.

Importantly, the language of small gestures is about thoughtfulness, not perfection. It's not about getting everything "right" but about showing that you care enough to try. Even a simple, heartfelt "thank you" for something your partner did—whether it's making dinner or taking out the trash—can have a profound impact. These moments of acknowledgment and appreciation create a culture of mutual respect and gratitude within the relationship.

Small gestures also have the power to bridge emotional distances. When life becomes hectic or disagreements arise, these acts of care can serve as reminders of the love and connection you share. A warm touch on the shoulder, a reassuring smile, or a small note left on the counter saying, "I love you and I'm here for you," can dissolve tension and rebuild closeness. These gestures remind your partner that, even in challenging times, your love remains steady.

In essence, small gestures are the daily love notes of a relationship. They don't require grand plans or extensive effort but are born from a genuine desire to connect and show care. By learning to recognize and practice the language of small gestures, couples can nurture a relationship that feels consistently loving, attentive, and meaningful.

As we move into the next section, we'll explore how these small acts of love can evolve into rituals of connection—habits and traditions that bring structure, comfort, and intimacy to your relationship.

Creating Rituals of Connection

Rituals are the heartbeat of a relationship, the consistent moments of connection that bring stability, comfort, and intimacy to daily life. While small gestures demonstrate care in spontaneous ways, rituals provide a predictable structure that strengthens the bond between partners. These shared habits—whether as simple as a morning coffee together or as meaningful as an annual getaway—become touchstones of connection, reinforcing the idea that love is built through time and presence.

Rituals of connection don't have to be elaborate. Often, the simplest traditions hold the most meaning. For instance, a couple might set aside 10 minutes every evening to talk about their day, sharing their thoughts, challenges, and triumphs. This ritual, while brief, fosters emotional intimacy by creating a space where both partners feel heard and valued. Over time, these moments become a source of comfort and reassurance, a reminder that no matter how busy life gets, their relationship remains a priority.

Shared rituals also strengthen bonds by creating a sense of teamwork and collaboration. For example, cooking dinner together every Sunday or going for a walk on Saturday mornings transforms routine activities into opportunities for connection. These rituals provide a sense of rhythm and predictability, helping couples feel grounded and in sync with one another. They also serve as a way to slow down and appreciate each other's presence in the midst of life's busyness.

Rituals can also be playful and creative, injecting joy and novelty into the relationship. Perhaps you create a quirky tradition, like making pancakes in funny shapes every weekend, or establish a game night where the winner gets to choose the next date activity. These lighthearted rituals not only bring laughter but also serve as a reminder of the unique bond you share. They celebrate the individuality of your partnership and the small, special ways you make life enjoyable together.

Seasonal or annual rituals provide another layer of connection. Celebrating anniversaries in meaningful ways, decorating the house together during the holidays, or planning a yearly trip to your favorite spot creates memories that become part of your relationship's story. These rituals offer moments to reflect on your journey as a couple, celebrate your growth, and look forward to what lies ahead.

Creating rituals of connection also helps couples navigate challenging times. During periods of stress or change, these rituals provide a sense of stability and continuity. For example, a couple might commit to having breakfast together every morning, even during a hectic week, as a way to stay connected. These moments act as anchors, reminding both partners of the strength of their bond and the support they offer each other.

Importantly, rituals of connection are not static—they evolve alongside the relationship. What starts as a weekly dinner date might shift into family movie nights as your lives and priorities change. The key is to remain intentional about creating and maintaining these rituals, ensuring they continue to meet the needs of both partners. Regularly discussing and adapting your rituals keeps them relevant and meaningful, allowing them to grow with you.

At their core, rituals of connection are about carving out intentional time to nurture the relationship. They serve as reminders that love requires effort and attention, not just on special occasions but in the everyday moments that make up your life together. By establishing these habits, couples create a foundation of stability, joy, and intimacy that sustains their relationship through all seasons.

As we move into the next section, we'll explore the art of appreciation and how recognizing and valuing the little things your partner does can deepen emotional bonds and foster a culture of gratitude within the relationship.

The Art of Appreciation

Appreciation is the quiet force that strengthens relationships and fosters a sense of belonging. It's the act of recognizing and valuing the little things your partner does—their efforts, gestures, and presence. While it may seem small, expressing gratitude regularly can have a profound impact on emotional intimacy and trust. The art of appreciation is about cultivating a culture of gratitude within your relationship, where both partners feel seen, valued, and cherished.

At its core, appreciation is an acknowledgment of effort. Whether it's noticing that your partner made the bed, cooked dinner, or simply remembered your favorite snack, expressing gratitude shows that you don't take their actions for granted. These small acknowledgments, like saying "Thank you for making breakfast" or "I really appreciated how you handled that situation," create a positive feedback loop that encourages more thoughtful gestures and strengthens your bond.

Appreciation also serves as a reminder of the good in your relationship, even during challenging times. It's easy to focus on frustrations or unmet expectations, but intentionally recognizing your partner's positive qualities shifts the perspective from criticism to admiration. For instance, instead of dwelling on an argument, you might reflect on how your partner supported you through a stressful situation or brought humor to an otherwise mundane day. This shift in focus fosters emotional safety and mutual respect.

Gratitude has a ripple effect in relationships. When one partner feels appreciated, they are more likely to reciprocate, creating a cycle of positivity and goodwill. For example, a simple "Thank you for listening to me today" can prompt your partner to express their own gratitude, further reinforcing the connection. Over time, this culture of mutual appreciation builds a foundation of trust and emotional intimacy.

One of the most effective ways to practice appreciation is to be specific. Generic statements like "Thanks for everything" are kind but lack the personal touch that makes gratitude feel meaningful. Instead, try highlighting something specific your partner did or a quality you admire. For example, "I love how patient you were when we were stuck in traffic" or "It meant so much to me that you remembered my favorite flowers." These moments of detailed acknowledgment show that you're paying attention and genuinely value their contributions.

Appreciation isn't just about words—it's also about actions. Small gestures, like leaving a note on the bathroom mirror, surprising your partner with their favorite treat, or taking on a task they usually handle, can speak volumes. These acts of thoughtfulness reinforce the message that you value your partner's efforts and are willing to reciprocate in kind. Actions, paired with verbal expressions of gratitude, create a powerful combination that deepens your emotional connection.

Over time, practicing appreciation strengthens emotional resilience within the relationship. Life's challenges can sometimes strain even the strongest partnerships, but gratitude acts as a buffer against negativity. When couples consistently express appreciation, they build a reservoir of positive feelings that helps them navigate difficult times. For instance, during an argument, the knowledge that your partner values and respects you can make it easier to approach the conflict with empathy and patience.

Appreciation also fosters self-esteem and confidence within the relationship. When you acknowledge your partner's efforts and qualities, you affirm their worth and their role in your life. This validation encourages them to continue investing in the relationship, knowing their contributions are recognized and valued. At the same time, expressing gratitude strengthens your own emotional connection to the relationship, reminding you of why you cherish your partner.

Ultimately, the art of appreciation is about creating a relationship where both partners feel valued, respected, and loved. It's not about grand declarations but the consistent acknowledgment of the little things that make your life together meaningful. By practicing gratitude daily, couples cultivate a sense of joy and connection that sustains them through both the ordinary and extraordinary moments of life.

As we move into the final section of this chapter, we'll explore how to sustain everyday romance over time, ensuring that these practices of thoughtfulness, gratitude, and connection remain a central part of your relationship no matter what stage you're in.

Sustaining Everyday Romance Over Time

Everyday romance is easy to nurture in the early stages of a relationship when everything feels new and exciting. However, as time passes, life's responsibilities, routines, and inevitable challenges can make it harder to maintain those small, thoughtful gestures. Sustaining everyday romance over the long term requires intentionality, creativity, and a willingness to prioritize your relationship, even amid life's busyness.

One of the most important aspects of sustaining romance is making it a conscious choice. Love doesn't thrive on autopilot—it requires effort and attention. Setting aside time to connect, no matter how busy your schedule gets, ensures that your relationship remains a priority. This doesn't mean carving out hours every day; even brief moments of connection, like a meaningful text or a quick embrace, can keep the spark alive. The key is consistency—showing your partner, day after day, that they matter to you.

Creativity also plays a vital role in maintaining everyday romance. As routines become established, it's easy to fall into habits that feel predictable or uninspired. Introducing small surprises, like planning an impromptu picnic, writing a heartfelt letter, or suggesting a new activity to try together, keeps the relationship dynamic. These gestures don't have to be elaborate; their impact lies in the thoughtfulness behind them. They remind your partner that you're still invested in keeping the relationship fresh and exciting.

Another way to sustain romance is to revisit the practices and rituals that brought you together in the first place.

Reflect on the early days of your relationship: What activities or gestures made you both feel connected and loved? Reintroducing those elements—whether it's a regular date night, a favorite hobby, or a shared playlist—can reignite the feelings of excitement and intimacy that marked the beginning of your journey together.

Overcoming complacency is another challenge couples face as relationships mature. It's natural to assume that your partner "just knows" how you feel, but this assumption can lead to a lack of communication and effort. To counteract this, make a point to express your love regularly and explicitly. Whether it's a simple "I love you," a compliment, or a note of appreciation, these affirmations keep the lines of connection open and ensure that your partner feels valued.

Sustaining everyday romance also involves adapting to life's changes. As careers evolve, families grow, and circumstances shift, the ways you express love may need to change as well. For example, a couple with young children might find that their romantic gestures shift from elaborate date nights to quieter moments of connection after the kids are asleep. Embracing these changes with flexibility and creativity allows romance to remain a constant presence, even as life evolves.

Communication is crucial in keeping everyday romance alive. Regularly checking in with your partner about their needs, feelings, and desires ensures that your efforts remain meaningful and aligned. Asking questions like "What makes you feel most loved?" or "Is there anything I can do to make you feel more connected?" fosters open dialogue and strengthens your ability to show care in ways that resonate with your partner.

Finally, sustaining everyday romance requires a mindset of gratitude and appreciation. By focusing on what's good and beautiful in your relationship, you create a positive emotional environment where love can flourish. Celebrating small victories, sharing laughter, and reflecting on your shared journey remind both partners of the joy they bring to each other's lives.

In the end, everyday romance isn't about grand gestures or perfection—it's about showing up for your partner with consistency, creativity, and care. By embracing these practices and making them a regular part of your relationship, you ensure that the love you share remains vibrant and fulfilling, no matter how much time passes or how life changes.

Everyday romance is the lifeblood of a lasting and fulfilling relationship. It's not the grand gestures or extravagant surprises that sustain love over time but the small, consistent acts of thoughtfulness, care, and connection. These moments remind us that love is a daily practice, one that thrives in the simple gestures—a warm smile, a kind word, or an unexpected note left on the counter.

This chapter has explored how small acts of love create a ripple effect that strengthens emotional bonds, fosters intimacy, and builds resilience. By understanding the science behind everyday romance, couples can see how these simple gestures are more than fleeting moments—they're investments in the relationship's long-term health. From learning the language of small gestures to creating meaningful rituals of connection, each act adds a thread to the rich tapestry of a shared life.

The art of appreciation emphasizes the importance of seeing and valuing your partner, not just for the big things they do but for the quiet, everyday efforts that make your life together richer. Gratitude, when expressed consistently, becomes the glue that holds a relationship together through both the ordinary and extraordinary moments of life.

Sustaining everyday romance over time requires intention, creativity, and adaptability. Life will inevitably bring changes, challenges, and routines, but the choice to prioritize love and connection ensures that romance remains a constant presence. Whether through a shared laugh, a comforting hug, or a playful surprise, these acts of love affirm the deep bond that holds you and your partner together.

As we move into the next chapter, which explores the role of adventure and thrill in relationships, remember that the foundation of love is built in the everyday. Adventure and passion may ignite the spark, but it's the quiet rhythm of daily romance that keeps the flame alive. By embracing the beauty of small gestures and the power of consistent care, couples create a love that not only endures but flourishes—one thoughtful act at a time.

The Future of Dating

The landscape of love is constantly shifting, shaped by advancements in technology, evolving cultural values, and the challenges of modern life. From dating apps that promise the perfect match to movements that emphasize emotional intelligence and self-awareness, the way we form connections is more dynamic than ever before. Yet, as the methods of meeting and bonding evolve, the core principles of love—trust, authenticity, and connection—remain timeless.

In this era of instant gratification and infinite choices, dating offers both unprecedented opportunities and unique challenges. Technology brings people together across distances, but it can also create barriers to genuine intimacy. Cultural shifts encourage inclusivity and emotional growth, yet they also challenge us to rethink traditional expectations and redefine success in relationships. Navigating this new landscape requires a blend of adaptability, clarity, and a deep understanding of what truly matters in love.

This chapter explores the future of dating, beginning with the profound impact of technology. How have apps, algorithms, and virtual experiences redefined the way we meet and connect? And what does it mean to strike a balance between digital tools and the human need for authentic, meaningful relationships? Let's dive into the new landscape of dating and the opportunities and complexities it brings.

Technology and the New Landscape of Dating

Technology has revolutionized the way we connect, and nowhere is this more evident than in the world of dating. From the rise of dating apps to AI-powered matchmaking and the potential of virtual reality, technology has opened doors to connections that were unimaginable just a few decades ago. However, these advancements come with their own set of complexities, as the digital world often challenges the authenticity and depth of human relationships.

Dating apps have become one of the most significant shifts in modern romance. With a simple swipe, users can access a seemingly endless pool of potential matches, breaking down geographical and social barriers. Apps like Tinder, Bumble, and Hinge have created opportunities for people to meet who might never have crossed paths otherwise. Yet, the convenience of these platforms often comes with the unintended consequence of fostering a "choice overload." When faced with so many options, individuals may struggle to commit, constantly wondering if there's someone better just a swipe away.

Artificial intelligence (AI) is also transforming the dating experience. Many platforms now use advanced algorithms to analyze user preferences, behavior, and personality traits to suggest compatible matches. These systems promise a more targeted and efficient way to find love, offering compatibility scores and tailored recommendations. However, AI-driven matchmaking raises questions about the role of intuition and chemistry in relationships. Can an algorithm truly predict the nuanced connection that forms when two people meet in person?

Virtual reality (VR) represents another frontier in the future of dating. Immersive platforms like VRChat are beginning to offer spaces where people can meet, interact, and even go on virtual dates. For long-distance couples, VR provides a way to bridge physical gaps, allowing partners to share experiences in a simulated environment. While these technologies bring exciting possibilities, they also highlight the need for balance between virtual interactions and real-world connections. Building a relationship entirely in a virtual space may lack the depth and authenticity of face-to-face interactions.

Social media further complicates modern dating. Platforms like Instagram, Facebook, and TikTok allow individuals to curate idealized versions of themselves, which can blur the lines between perception and reality. Couples may struggle with issues like comparison, public validation, and miscommunication, all of which are amplified by the pressures of maintaining a digital presence. At the same time, social media can also serve as a powerful tool for staying connected and expressing love, particularly in long-distance relationships.

Striking a balance between technology and genuine human connection is one of the biggest challenges of modern dating. While apps and algorithms can facilitate introductions, the deeper work of building a relationship still requires vulnerability, communication, and emotional presence. Technology can enhance the dating experience, but it's essential to approach it as a tool, not a substitute, for authentic connection.

The new landscape of dating offers incredible opportunities but also demands intentionality. By understanding how technology influences our relationships and choosing to use it thoughtfully, we can navigate this digital age without losing sight of the timeless values that define meaningful love. As we move forward, the challenge lies in leveraging these advancements while preserving the human heart at the core of every relationship.

The Evolving Role of Values and Intentions

As the dating landscape evolves, so do the values and intentions that guide how people approach relationships. Unlike past generations, where traditional expectations often dictated the path to love, today's daters are redefining what it means to connect and commit. Equality, inclusivity, emotional health, and personal growth have taken center stage, influencing how relationships are formed and sustained. This shift marks a move toward intentional dating, where authenticity and shared values replace outdated societal norms.

Generational attitudes play a significant role in this evolution. Millennials and Gen Z, in particular, are reshaping the dating narrative by prioritizing emotional intelligence and mutual respect. For many, dating is no longer about adhering to a prescribed timeline of courtship, marriage, and family. Instead, it's about fostering connections that align with individual goals and aspirations. This focus on compatibility and shared purpose ensures that relationships feel more authentic and fulfilling, even if they don't follow traditional scripts.

Intentional dating has also gained prominence as more people reject casual flings in favor of deeper, more meaningful connections. For example, dating apps like Hinge position themselves as "designed to be deleted," emphasizing the importance of finding long-term compatibility rather than endless swiping. This approach reflects a broader cultural trend toward mindfulness in relationships, where individuals are encouraged to align their actions with their values and aspirations.

Inclusivity is another driving force behind this shift. Modern dating culture places a growing emphasis on embracing diversity, whether in terms of race, gender, sexuality, or lifestyle. Daters are increasingly aware of the importance of creating spaces where everyone feels seen, valued, and respected. This shift not only broadens opportunities for connection but also encourages individuals to challenge their own biases and expand their perspectives.

Mental health awareness has further shaped dating priorities. Today's daters are more likely to prioritize emotional well-being, both for themselves and their partners. Open conversations about therapy, boundaries, and personal growth have become normalized, fostering healthier and more supportive relationships. For instance, a couple might openly discuss their communication styles or coping mechanisms, ensuring they can navigate challenges with empathy and understanding. This focus on emotional health ensures that relationships are built on a foundation of trust and mutual care.

The evolving role of values has also redefined what success looks like in a relationship. Traditionally, success was often measured by milestones like engagement, marriage, and children. Now, success is viewed through a more personalized lens—one that prioritizes happiness, growth, and mutual fulfillment. For some couples, this might mean pursuing a long-term partnership without formalizing it through marriage. For others, it could mean co-parenting while maintaining separate households. This flexibility allows individuals to design relationships that truly reflect their needs and desires.

At its core, this shift toward values-based and intentional dating emphasizes authenticity. Rather than conforming to societal expectations, modern daters are encouraged to focus on what feels right for them. This approach not only leads to stronger, more meaningful connections but also empowers individuals to approach love with confidence and clarity.

As the dating landscape continues to evolve, these shifts in values and intentions will likely shape the future of relationships. By prioritizing emotional health, inclusivity, and authenticity, today's daters are laying the groundwork for a more thoughtful and fulfilling approach to love. In the next section, we'll explore how modern challenges—like social media and the pressures of a fast-paced world—impact dating and how couples can navigate these complexities with resilience and adaptability.

Overcoming Modern Challenges in Dating

Dating in today's world comes with unique challenges. While technology and evolving values have opened up exciting opportunities, they've also introduced complexities that can make building meaningful connections more difficult. From the pressures of social media to the impact of modern stressors like burnout and comparison culture, navigating these obstacles requires resilience, adaptability, and intentionality.

One of the most significant modern challenges is the influence of social media on relationships. Platforms like Instagram, TikTok, and Facebook allow individuals to curate idealized versions of their lives, often blurring the lines between reality and perception. In the context of dating, this can lead to unhealthy comparisons, where individuals feel pressured to measure their relationships against the seemingly perfect ones they see online. A simple post of a romantic dinner or an anniversary surprise can inadvertently trigger feelings of inadequacy or insecurity, even in a happy relationship.

Moreover, social media often creates unrealistic expectations for communication and validation. The immediacy of platforms like texting and messaging can lead to misunderstandings when responses are delayed or tone is misinterpreted. Additionally, the pressure to publicly display affection—through posts, comments, or couple photos—can detract from the authenticity of private moments. Striking a balance between sharing your relationship and keeping it sacred requires intentionality and clear communication with your partner about boundaries.

Another challenge modern couples face is the impact of burnout and stress on dating. With demanding careers, packed schedules, and the ever-present pressure to "do it all," finding time and energy for meaningful connection can feel daunting. This is especially true for individuals navigating online dating, where swiping fatigue and ghosting have become common experiences. The emotional toll of these patterns can leave individuals feeling discouraged or disengaged, making it harder to approach dating with optimism.

Mental health challenges have also become more prevalent in modern dating, partly due to the fast pace of life and societal pressures. Anxiety, depression, and self-doubt can create barriers to forming and maintaining healthy relationships. For instance, someone struggling with anxiety may find it difficult to open up emotionally or feel confident in their interactions, while a partner dealing with stress might unintentionally withdraw from the relationship. Addressing these challenges requires compassion, self-awareness, and a commitment to prioritizing emotional well-being—for both yourself and your partner.

The abundance of choice in modern dating adds another layer of complexity. Apps and online platforms offer seemingly endless options, but this can lead to a phenomenon known as choice overload. When faced with too many possibilities, individuals may struggle to commit, constantly wondering if there's someone better just a swipe away. This mindset not only creates anxiety but can also prevent meaningful connections from forming, as people hesitate to invest in relationships for fear of missing out on a "better" match.

To overcome these challenges, intentionality is key. For example, couples can combat the negative effects of social media by focusing on private, meaningful moments rather than external validation. Taking intentional breaks from technology or agreeing on boundaries for online interactions can help preserve the authenticity of the relationship. Similarly, addressing stress and burnout may involve setting aside dedicated time for connection, such as unplugged date nights or weekend getaways that allow partners to recharge together.

Self-awareness and communication are also essential tools for navigating modern challenges. Being honest about your needs, boundaries, and feelings creates a foundation of trust and understanding. For instance, if one partner feels overwhelmed by work, openly discussing how they can reconnect as a couple helps prevent misunderstandings and resentment. Similarly, being transparent about mental health struggles allows partners to support each other in meaningful ways.

Ultimately, overcoming modern challenges in dating requires a balance of resilience and adaptability. While the pressures of social media, stress, and choice overload may feel overwhelming, they also provide opportunities for growth and connection. By approaching these challenges with intentionality, couples can build stronger, more fulfilling relationships that thrive in the face of modern complexities.

In the next section, we'll explore how a return to authenticity—focusing on offline connections and genuine interactions—can help counteract the challenges of the digital age and create deeper, more meaningful bonds.

The Return to Authenticity

In an age dominated by technology and fast-paced communication, there's a growing movement toward authenticity in relationships. People are increasingly recognizing the limitations of digital interactions and seeking ways to connect on a deeper, more genuine level. The return to authenticity emphasizes the importance of being fully present, emotionally available, and vulnerable in relationships—qualities that are often overshadowed by the convenience and speed of modern dating.

One of the key aspects of this shift is the renewed appreciation for offline connections. While dating apps and social media have made it easier to meet new people, they can also create a sense of detachment, as interactions often lack the depth and spontaneity of face-to-face encounters. More and more individuals are stepping away from screens to explore organic ways of meeting potential partners, such as joining interest-based groups, attending community events, or simply being open to conversations in everyday settings. These offline interactions allow people to form connections based on shared experiences and genuine chemistry, rather than curated profiles or algorithms.

The return to authenticity also challenges the "highlight reel" culture of social media, where people often present idealized versions of themselves. Authenticity requires embracing imperfections and being comfortable showing up as your true self. For example, rather than focusing on crafting the perfect first impression, individuals are learning to value honesty and vulnerability in their interactions. Sharing your fears, dreams, and quirks may feel risky, but it creates a foundation of trust and emotional intimacy that is essential for meaningful relationships.

Presence is another cornerstone of authentic connection. In a world filled with distractions, being fully engaged in the moment can be a powerful way to show love and respect. Whether it's putting away your phone during a date, actively listening to your partner, or simply spending quality time together without interruptions, these acts of presence demonstrate that you value the relationship and are committed to nurturing it. Authenticity thrives in these quiet, undistracted moments, where both partners can truly see and appreciate each other.

The pursuit of authenticity also encourages individuals to prioritize emotional availability. Many modern daters struggle with fears of vulnerability or commitment, often keeping potential partners at arm's length. Authenticity requires breaking down these barriers and approaching relationships with openness and a willingness to connect deeply. This means being honest about your intentions, expressing your feelings without fear of judgment, and showing empathy and understanding when your partner does the same.

Focusing on quality over quantity is another way the return to authenticity is reshaping modern dating. In an age of endless choices, it's tempting to prioritize breadth over depth, swiping through countless profiles or juggling multiple matches at once. However, authenticity invites a slower, more intentional approach. Taking the time to truly get to know someone—investing in conversations, shared experiences, and mutual growth—leads to deeper, more fulfilling connections. This shift away from instant gratification allows relationships to develop organically, without the pressure of constant comparison or the fear of missing out.

The return to authenticity also highlights the importance of meaningful actions over performative gestures. Rather than focusing on grand displays of romance, couples are learning to appreciate the smaller, more personal ways they show care for each other. A handwritten note, a heartfelt apology, or a quiet moment of support during a tough day speaks volumes about the depth of a relationship. These thoughtful acts create a sense of emotional safety and connection, allowing love to flourish in its most genuine form.

Ultimately, the return to authenticity is about rediscovering what makes love meaningful. It's a reminder that relationships thrive not on perfection or performance but on honesty, presence, and mutual respect. By prioritizing authenticity, individuals can build connections that feel real, fulfilling, and deeply rooted in mutual understanding.

In the next section, we'll explore the growing importance of self-discovery in modern dating and how personal growth enhances the quality of our relationships.

The Role of Self-Discovery in the Future of Love

In the ever-evolving landscape of dating, one truth remains constant: the quality of our relationships is deeply tied to the relationship we have with ourselves. Self-discovery has become a central theme in modern dating, as individuals increasingly prioritize personal growth, self-awareness, and emotional intelligence as prerequisites for meaningful connections. The journey of understanding who you are, what you value, and what you need in a partner lays the foundation for a relationship built on authenticity and mutual respect.

At the heart of self-discovery is the ability to reflect on your past experiences and patterns. By taking the time to examine previous relationships—both their successes and challenges—you gain valuable insights into your needs, boundaries, and triggers. For instance, someone who has experienced miscommunication in the past might realize the importance of prioritizing clear and honest dialogue in future relationships. This level of introspection not only helps individuals grow but also equips them to approach dating with clarity and purpose.

Self-awareness is another cornerstone of self-discovery in dating. Understanding your emotional triggers, strengths, and areas for growth allows you to show up in relationships with greater empathy and vulnerability. For example, recognizing that you tend to withdraw during conflict gives you the opportunity to work on more constructive ways of addressing challenges. Similarly, being aware of your love language enables you to communicate your needs effectively while also understanding how to meet your partner's. This level of emotional intelligence fosters deeper connection and minimizes misunderstandings.

Modern dating also places a greater emphasis on personal values and compatibility. The journey of self-discovery often involves identifying the core principles that guide your life, such as integrity, ambition, or creativity. These values serve as a compass in choosing a partner whose priorities align with your own. For instance, someone who values adventure and spontaneity may seek a partner who shares their enthusiasm for exploring the world. By knowing what matters most to you, you can create relationships that feel authentic and fulfilling.

Another important aspect of self-discovery is learning to embrace your individuality. In the past, relationships were often viewed as a merging of identities, with one or both partners sacrificing their personal aspirations for the sake of the partnership. Today, the focus has shifted toward maintaining individuality while fostering connection. This means pursuing your passions, hobbies, and goals, even as you invest in a relationship. By nurturing your sense of self, you bring a richer, more balanced perspective to the partnership, allowing both you and your partner to thrive.

Self-discovery also involves addressing emotional baggage and healing past wounds. Carrying unresolved issues into a relationship can create barriers to intimacy and trust. By taking the time to process and work through these challenges—whether through therapy, mindfulness practices, or journaling—you free yourself to approach love with an open heart and a clear mind. For example, someone who has experienced betrayal in the past might focus on rebuilding trust within themselves before seeking it in a partner. This inner work not only enhances your emotional well-being but also strengthens your ability to build a healthy, secure relationship.

The journey of self-discovery is not a one-time event; it's an ongoing process that evolves as you grow and change. As life presents new experiences and challenges, your understanding of yourself deepens, allowing you to approach relationships with renewed perspective. For instance, someone entering a new phase of life—such as parenthood or a career change—may find that their priorities and needs shift. By remaining curious and open to self-reflection, you ensure that your relationships continue to align with who you are becoming.

Ultimately, the role of self-discovery in the future of love is about creating relationships that are grounded in authenticity, mutual respect, and emotional growth. By knowing and loving yourself first, you build a strong foundation for connections that feel meaningful and fulfilling. As the dating landscape continues to evolve, this commitment to self-awareness and personal growth will remain a timeless and essential part of building lasting relationships.

The future of dating is as exciting as it is complex, blending modern tools and shifting values with the timeless principles of connection and authenticity. As we've explored throughout this chapter, the evolving landscape of relationships offers both incredible opportunities and unique challenges. From leveraging technology thoughtfully to prioritizing personal growth, the way we approach love is continually transforming, creating new pathways for meaningful connections.

Technology has undeniably reshaped how we meet and interact, bringing both convenience and complications. While apps, algorithms, and virtual platforms open doors to possibilities that were once unimaginable, they also demand intentionality to ensure that genuine human connection remains at the heart of our relationships. By balancing the advantages of digital tools with the need for offline presence, couples can foster relationships that are both innovative and deeply rooted in authenticity.

The evolving values of modern dating—such as inclusivity, emotional intelligence, and intentionality—reflect a collective desire for deeper, more fulfilling relationships. These shifts encourage individuals to approach love with mindfulness and clarity, breaking free from outdated societal expectations and redefining success in ways that align with personal growth and happiness.

At the same time, modern challenges like social media pressures, burnout, and choice overload remind us of the importance of resilience and adaptability. By setting boundaries, focusing on quality over quantity, and fostering open communication, couples can navigate these complexities with grace and intention, ensuring that their connections remain strong and enduring.

Perhaps the most profound shift in the future of dating is the emphasis on self-discovery. As individuals invest in understanding their own needs, values, and aspirations, they bring a deeper sense of authenticity and purpose to their relationships. This journey of personal growth not only enhances the quality of their connections but also creates a foundation for love that is both resilient and transformative.

As we look ahead, the future of love calls for a balance between embracing innovation and honoring the fundamental truths of human connection. While technology, values, and societal norms may continue to evolve, the essence of love—trust, vulnerability, and presence—remains timeless. By approaching dating with intention, authenticity, and an open heart, individuals can build relationships that are not only meaningful in the present but also enduring in the face of the future.

In the next and final chapter, we will reflect on the lessons learned throughout this journey, exploring how the principles of meaningful connection, adventure, and romance come together to create a fulfilling and lasting relationship. The future of dating isn't just about trends or tools—it's about creating love stories that stand the test of time.

Crafting a Love That Lasts

As we come to the final chapter, it's time to reflect on the journey we've taken—exploring the fundamentals of dating, the psychology of connection, the role of adventure and romance, and the evolving landscape of relationships. Throughout this book, one truth has remained central: love is not a destination but an ongoing journey. It is shaped by moments of vulnerability, effort, and discovery, woven together by the choices we make every day. Chapter 11 ties together the lessons we've learned, offering a final reflection on how to create a meaningful, lasting relationship that thrives in the face of life's changes.

Revisiting the Core Principles

Love, at its heart, is both beautifully simple and deeply complex. While each relationship is unique, certain principles serve as universal truths—cornerstones that support lasting connections. As we reflect on the journey through this book, it becomes clear that the foundations of communication, vulnerability, and shared growth are essential to crafting a love that endures the test of time.

Communication is the lifeline of any relationship. It's not just about talking but about truly understanding and being understood. Open, honest dialogue creates a safe space where partners can express their needs, fears, and desires without fear of judgment. Reflect on the moments when communication has deepened your bond—whether it's a heartfelt conversation during a quiet evening or a shared laugh over a silly misunderstanding. These exchanges, however small, are the threads that weave connection into everyday life. Active listening, empathy, and the willingness to engage in meaningful dialogue form the bedrock of emotional intimacy.

Vulnerability is another pillar of a strong relationship. It's in those moments of raw honesty—when you reveal your insecurities, dreams, or past hurts—that true connection is formed. Vulnerability requires courage, but it also fosters trust and emotional safety. When you allow yourself to be seen and accepted as you are, and when you extend the same grace to your partner, you build a relationship rooted in authenticity. Reflect on the times you've opened up to your partner or supported them in their own moments of vulnerability. These experiences are not just milestones but the glue that holds your bond together.

The third principle, shared growth, reminds us that love is a journey, not a fixed state. Healthy relationships are dynamic, evolving as both partners grow individually and together. This requires a willingness to adapt, learn, and support each other's aspirations. Growth doesn't mean always moving at the same pace or in the same direction—it's about finding ways to align your paths while honoring each other's individuality. Think back on the ways you and your partner have supported each other's goals, overcome challenges, or celebrated milestones. These moments of growth are testaments to the strength of your partnership.

Yet, these principles are not stand-alone concepts—they are interconnected. Communication enables vulnerability, vulnerability deepens intimacy, and intimacy creates the foundation for shared growth. Together, they form a cycle that sustains love over time. The beauty of these principles lies in their accessibility: they don't require grand gestures or perfect circumstances. They thrive in the everyday acts of care, effort, and intention.

As we revisit these core principles, it's important to remember that relationships are not static. They require constant nurturing, reflection, and effort. By prioritizing communication, embracing vulnerability, and committing to shared growth, couples can build a love that not only endures but flourishes. These principles serve as a reminder that the essence of love is found in the daily choices we make to connect, support, and cherish one another.

In the next section, we'll explore the dynamic nature of love—how it evolves over time and how couples can balance routine and novelty to keep their relationship vibrant and fulfilling.

The Dynamic Nature of Love

Love is not a fixed state—it is a living, breathing entity that evolves with time. As relationships progress, they transition through stages, each bringing its own challenges and rewards. The dynamic nature of love calls for adaptability, creativity, and the ability to embrace both change and consistency. By understanding and honoring this evolution, couples can keep their connection vibrant, resilient, and deeply fulfilling.

One of the most important aspects of love's evolution is the balance between routine and novelty. Routines provide a sense of stability and predictability, forming the foundation of a secure partnership. Simple habits like sharing morning coffee, regular date nights, or weekly check-ins create a rhythm that keeps couples grounded. These rituals remind partners that they can rely on each other, even amid life's uncertainties. However, routine alone is not enough to sustain the excitement and passion that make love thrive.

Novelty, on the other hand, injects energy and curiosity into a relationship. Trying new activities, exploring unfamiliar places, or simply breaking out of the ordinary can reignite the spark of excitement that first drew partners together. For example, surprising your partner with an impromptu weekend getaway or signing up for a dance class together can create shared memories that strengthen your bond. Novelty reminds couples that there is always more to discover about each other and the world, keeping the relationship dynamic and forward-focused.

The key is to find harmony between these two forces. Too much routine can lead to stagnation, while constant novelty can feel overwhelming or unsustainable. A healthy relationship blends the comfort of familiar rituals with the thrill of new experiences. For instance, a couple might revisit their favorite restaurant but order a dish they've never tried or take their usual evening walk but add a twist, like discussing childhood memories or stargazing along the way. These small shifts keep the relationship fresh without sacrificing the stability that routine provides.

The dynamic nature of love also requires embracing change as an inevitable part of life. Over time, partners grow as individuals, and their relationship must adapt to these changes. Whether it's career transitions, parenthood, or personal development, each new phase brings opportunities to deepen the connection. Rather than resisting change, couples can view it as a chance to learn more about each other and navigate challenges together. For example, adjusting to a partner's new work schedule might involve creating new rituals of connection, like cooking dinner together on weekends or scheduling regular calls during travel.

Adapting to change also means recognizing that love itself can take on different forms over time. The infatuation of early romance may give way to a deeper, more enduring bond characterized by trust, respect, and companionship. This shift is not a loss but an evolution—a testament to the relationship's resilience and maturity. By appreciating each stage of love for what it offers, couples can find joy and meaning in every chapter of their journey.

Conflict is another area where the dynamic nature of love comes into play. Disagreements are a natural part of any relationship, but how couples navigate them determines the strength of their bond. Viewing conflict as an opportunity for growth rather than a threat allows partners to address issues constructively. Open communication, empathy, and a willingness to compromise transform challenges into moments of connection. For instance, resolving a disagreement about household responsibilities might lead to a clearer division of tasks and a renewed sense of teamwork.

Ultimately, the dynamic nature of love is what makes it so enriching. By embracing both routine and novelty, adapting to life's changes, and viewing challenges as opportunities, couples create a relationship that grows stronger with time. Love's evolution is a reminder that no matter how much a relationship changes, its essence—mutual care, respect, and connection—remains constant.

As we move into the next section, we'll explore the role of individual growth in relationships and how nurturing your sense of self enhances the quality and depth of your connection.

The Role of Individual Growth

While a strong relationship thrives on connection and shared experiences, its foundation is often built on the personal growth of each individual. Nurturing your own aspirations, emotional health, and sense of identity not only enriches your life but also strengthens your partnership. Individual growth allows you to bring your best self to the relationship, fostering a deeper connection and creating space for mutual respect and support.

At the heart of individual growth is self-awareness. Understanding your emotions, triggers, and desires enables you to communicate effectively and approach your relationship with clarity. For example, recognizing your need for personal downtime after a busy day allows you to set boundaries without causing misunderstandings. Similarly, being aware of your strengths and areas for improvement encourages you to work on yourself, which benefits both you and your partner. A relationship built on two self-aware individuals is more likely to thrive because both partners can articulate their needs and support each other's growth.

Personal growth also involves pursuing your passions and goals, independent of the relationship. While it's natural to share many aspects of your life with your partner, maintaining your individuality ensures that you remain a well-rounded person with interests, skills, and ambitions outside the partnership. For instance, taking a class, pursuing a hobby, or dedicating time to a career goal shows your partner that you value self-improvement. This not only enriches your life but also inspires your partner to pursue their own growth, creating a dynamic where both individuals are continuously evolving.

Growth is also about emotional resilience. Life inevitably brings challenges, and your ability to navigate them as an individual impacts your relationship. Developing healthy coping mechanisms, such as mindfulness, therapy, or journaling, allows you to manage stress and communicate effectively with your partner during difficult times. For example, if you're facing a career setback, taking the time to process your emotions and reflect on your next steps helps you avoid projecting frustration onto your relationship. This emotional maturity fosters a sense of stability and trust.

Relationships often serve as mirrors, reflecting areas where personal growth is needed. Conflicts or recurring patterns in your partnership can reveal unresolved issues or insecurities that stem from your past. Embracing these moments as opportunities for self-reflection allows you to break negative cycles and build healthier dynamics. For instance, if you notice a tendency to avoid difficult conversations, working on your communication skills can transform your relationship and enhance your confidence in other areas of life.

Individual growth also reinforces the importance of self-care. Prioritizing your physical, mental, and emotional well-being ensures that you have the energy and presence to invest in your relationship. Simple practices like exercising, eating well, and setting aside time for relaxation create a solid foundation for your overall happiness. When you care for yourself, you model healthy behaviors for your partner and contribute to a relationship that feels balanced and nurturing.

Mutual support is key to fostering growth within a relationship. While personal development is an individual journey, a loving partnership provides encouragement and accountability. Celebrating each other's achievements, offering guidance during challenges, and showing genuine interest in each other's goals creates a sense of teamwork. For example, if your partner decides to pursue a career change, being their cheerleader through the ups and downs strengthens your bond while reinforcing their confidence.

Importantly, individual growth doesn't mean growing apart. On the contrary, it allows you to bring new perspectives, skills, and energy into the relationship. As both partners evolve, they contribute to a dynamic where the relationship itself becomes a space for learning and discovery. This mutual evolution ensures that your connection remains vibrant, meaningful, and deeply fulfilling.

Ultimately, the role of individual growth in a relationship is about balance. By nurturing yourself while supporting your partner, you create a partnership that is both rooted in shared values and enriched by personal aspirations. In the next section, we'll explore how a shared vision and aligned goals can further strengthen the foundation of a lasting relationship.

The Power of Shared Vision

A shared vision is the guiding light of any strong relationship. It represents the alignment of values, goals, and dreams that both partners work toward together. While love forms the emotional core of a relationship, a shared vision provides the practical framework that keeps it focused, purposeful, and enduring. By creating and nurturing a common path, couples can navigate life's complexities with a sense of unity and direction.

At its foundation, a shared vision begins with aligned values. These are the principles that guide how each partner approaches life, such as honesty, compassion, ambition, or family. While no two individuals will agree on everything, having a core set of shared values ensures that both partners are working toward a relationship that feels authentic and meaningful. For instance, a couple who values adventure might prioritize travel and exploration, while partners who emphasize stability may focus on building a strong home life. Recognizing and celebrating these shared values creates a foundation of trust and mutual understanding.

Open communication is essential for creating and maintaining a shared vision. Partners must be willing to discuss their individual goals, aspirations, and concerns, ensuring that their paths align in meaningful ways. For example, conversations about career ambitions, family planning, or financial priorities allow couples to identify areas of overlap and potential challenges. These discussions, when approached with honesty and empathy, not only clarify the relationship's direction but also deepen emotional intimacy.

A shared vision also involves collaborative goal-setting. By working together to establish short-term and long-term goals, couples create a sense of partnership and accountability. For instance, setting a goal to save for a home, plan a major trip, or support each other's educational pursuits transforms individual dreams into joint endeavors. This collaboration fosters a sense of teamwork, reminding both partners that they are stronger together than apart.

Importantly, a shared vision doesn't mean sacrificing individuality. While it emphasizes alignment, it also allows space for personal growth and exploration. Each partner's unique aspirations can coexist with the couple's collective goals, creating a dynamic where both individuals feel supported and fulfilled. For example, one partner might pursue a demanding career while the other focuses on creative projects, but both work together to ensure that their shared priorities—such as quality time or financial planning—are honored.

Flexibility is another key component of a shared vision. Life is unpredictable, and circumstances often require adjustments to previously established plans. Whether it's a sudden job relocation, a change in health, or an unexpected opportunity, the ability to adapt ensures that the relationship remains resilient. A strong shared vision isn't rigid—it evolves alongside the couple, reflecting their growth and changing priorities. For example, a couple who initially planned to travel extensively might shift their focus to creating a home base when they decide to start a family. These shifts, when navigated with mutual respect and understanding, strengthen the bond rather than weaken it.

The power of a shared vision also lies in its ability to create a sense of legacy. Partners who work toward common dreams often leave a lasting impact, whether through the family they build, the community they support, or the goals they achieve together. This sense of purpose adds depth to the relationship, transforming it into something larger than the sum of its parts. For instance, a couple who volunteers together or supports a cause they're passionate about not only strengthens their connection but also contributes to a shared legacy of meaning and impact.

Ultimately, a shared vision is about building a life that feels intentional and aligned. It ensures that both partners are moving forward with clarity, purpose, and a sense of togetherness. By fostering open communication, setting collaborative goals, and embracing flexibility, couples can create a partnership that is both deeply fulfilling and enduring.

As we conclude this chapter, we'll tie together the themes of love, growth, and connection, reflecting on how these elements combine to craft a relationship that stands the test of time.

Crafting a Love That Stands the Test of Time

As we bring this chapter to a close, it's clear that the journey of love is one of intention, growth, and connection. Each element we've explored—core principles, the dynamic nature of love, individual growth, and the power of a shared vision—forms an integral part of a relationship that not only endures but thrives. Together, these elements remind us that love is not a single milestone but an ongoing process of discovery and effort.

At its core, love is built on communication, vulnerability, and shared growth. These timeless principles create a foundation of trust and emotional intimacy, ensuring that both partners feel seen, heard, and valued. By prioritizing these practices, couples can navigate challenges and celebrate joys with confidence and mutual support. Communication fosters understanding, vulnerability deepens connection, and shared growth keeps the relationship dynamic and forward-focused.

The dynamic nature of love calls on us to embrace change with openness and adaptability. As life evolves, so too do relationships. By balancing the comfort of routine with the excitement of novelty, couples can keep their connection vibrant and fulfilling. Whether it's revisiting cherished traditions or exploring new experiences together, this balance ensures that love remains both stable and exciting, even in the face of life's unpredictability.

Individual growth serves as the heartbeat of a thriving partnership. By nurturing your own aspirations, self-awareness, and emotional health, you bring your best self to the relationship. At the same time, supporting your partner's journey of growth creates a dynamic where both individuals can flourish. This balance of individuality and connection ensures that the relationship remains a source of inspiration, strength, and mutual respect.

A shared vision ties it all together, providing direction and purpose. When couples align their values, goals, and dreams, they create a partnership that feels intentional and united. This vision evolves with time, reflecting the growth and changing priorities of the relationship. It provides both a roadmap and a legacy, transforming love into a journey of shared meaning and fulfillment.

Ultimately, crafting a love that stands the test of time is about blending these elements into a cohesive whole. It's about showing up every day with intention, care, and a willingness to grow—both as individuals and as partners. It's about finding joy in the small, everyday moments while embracing the bigger picture of a life built together. Love, in its truest form, is a partnership where two people choose each other again and again, creating a relationship that is both enduring and extraordinary.

As we move into the book's final reflections, we'll look back on the lessons learned and explore how they come together to inspire and guide the relationships we cultivate. The journey doesn't end here; it continues in the choices, moments, and connections that shape your story of love.

The Lasting Impression

A **Love Letter to Love**

As you close this book, I hope you walk away with more than just ideas for dates. I hope you carry the spark of curiosity that kindled your desire to connect, the courage to be vulnerable, and the understanding that great relationships are not found—they are made.

The beauty of a date is not in its grandeur or perfection but in its intention. It's the laughter shared over a simple meal, the warmth of a hand held on a quiet evening, the joy of discovering a new side of someone you thought you already knew.

Love, at its core, is a series of moments. Some are fleeting; others will leave a mark so deep that they shape who you are. Whether you're planning a first date or your hundredth, remember this: it's not about what you do, but the meaning you create together.

So go forth, not just as a curator of dates, but as an artist of connection. May you find the courage to create, the grace to forgive, and the joy to love—again and again.

This is not the end of your journey; it's a new beginning. Love well, live fully, and never stop curating a life that makes your heart beat a little faster.

With all my heart,
Ethan Starke

Your Chapter

www.ingramcontent.com/pod-product-compliance
Lightning Source LLC
Chambersburg PA
CBHW020539030426
42337CB00013B/910